NECESSARY INCLUSION

Embracing the Changing Faces of Technology

Much continued
success !

Anis Yates Rivers

NECESSARY INCLUSION

Embracing the Changing Faces
of Technology

AVIS YATES RIVERS

HenschelHAUS Publishing, Inc.
Milwaukee, Wisconsin

Published by
HenschelHAUS Publishing, Inc.
www.henschelHAUSbooks.com

PB-ISBN: 97159598-517-0 (paperback)
HC-ISBN: 978159598-518-7 (hardcover)
E-ISBN: 978159598-519-4
LCCN: 2016961709

Publisher's Cataloging-In-Publication Data
(Prepared by The Donohue Group, Inc.)
Names: Rivers, Avis Yates.
Title: Necessary inclusion : embracing the changing faces of technology / Avis Yates Rivers.
Description: Milwaukee, Wisconsin : HenschelHAUS Publishing, Inc., [2016]
Identifiers: LCCN 2016961709 | ISBN 978-1-59598-517-0 (paperback) | ISBN 978-1-59598-518-7 (hardcover) | ISBN 978-1-59598-519-4 (ebook)
Subjects: LCSH: Women in technology. | Minorities in technology. | Information technology--Vocational guidance. | Women computer scientists.
Classification: LCC T36 .R58 2016 (print) | LCC T36 (ebook) | DDC 604.82--dc23

Author photos by Keith Major Photography, NYC
Author's creative direction by Mikki Taylor and Satin Doll Productions
Cover design by Zomona Brown

Printed in the United States of America

To all the change agents
in the world working diligently
to ensure the meaningful participation of
girls, women, and people of color
in technology and leadership.

TABLE OF CONTENTS

FOREWORD

Women, and especially women of color, are essentially "absent" from inventing technology. Today, only 19 percent of all software developers are female. Of that 19 percent, very few are found in technology leadership roles that would enable them to make truly innovative contributions. These and other statistics imply that a largely homogeneous group is creating the technology the world uses today—U.S. white males (and increasingly, Asian males).

When women do make technical contributions, they are often ignored, not recognized, or not given credit for their ideas. This is especially troubling given ample evidence of the critical benefits diversity brings to innovation, problem-solving, and creativity. Indeed, innovation springs from diversity—diversity of ideas, perspectives, voices, and in short, a diversity of people. A solid body of research in computing and in other fields documents the enhanced performance outcomes when a diverse range of women are present in meaningful and creative roles.

Many social and cultural influences increasingly impede women's contributions to technical creation in today's tech workforce. Recognizing women as technical contributors requires explicit, conscious effort—not just unconscious bias training. Simply adding women to the roles for the purpose of inflating the numbers is not going to make their ideas valued or used.

Technical design teams need to employ strategies and techniques for making sure ideas are heard and discussed. Managers and supervisors (both men and women) need to serve as champions for their female technologists. And they need to be informed and equipped to do so effectively, with a clear understanding of both the values and unique challenges to gender inclusion embedded in our current systems and operations.

A pressing need to address these factors led to the formation of the National Center for Women & Information Technology (NCWIT) in 2004, a National Science Foundation-funded effort to "significantly increase women's meaningful participation in computing." We stressed "significantly" because clearly, the numbers were quite low then and "meaningful" because this effort was not intended to be merely a numbers game.

We must have women in the roles critical to the invention of future technology (architect, lead designer, etc.) and not only in the jobs that support those who create it (such as project management and system verification).

WHY DOES ADDRESSING WOMEN'S ABSENCE MATTER?

DIVERSITY BRINGS SIGNIFICANT BENEFITS TO TECHNICAL INNOVATION

Women's current underrepresentation spells trouble for the tech industry and for the future of technical innovation, especially in light of an increasing body

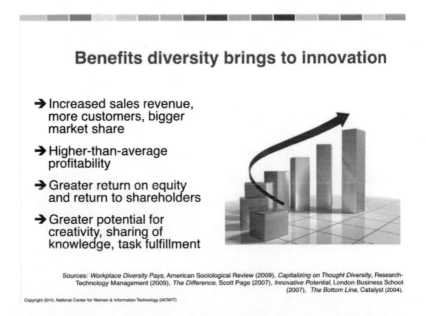

Benefits diversity brings to innovation

➔ Increased sales revenue, more customers, bigger market share

➔ Higher-than-average profitability

➔ Greater return on equity and return to shareholders

➔ Greater potential for creativity, sharing of knowledge, task fulfillment

Sources: *Workplace Diversity Pays*, American Sociological Review (2009), *Capitalizing on Thought Diversity*, Research-Technology Management (2009), *The Difference*, Scott Page (2007), *Innovative Potential*, London Business School (2007), *The Bottom Line*, Catalyst (2004).

Copyright 2010, National Center for Women & Information Technology (NCWIT)

of research documenting the significant benefits that diversity brings to innovation. Some of these key benefits are summarized in the figure below.

Let's consider a few examples from specific studies:

A study (Herring, 2009) of 500 U.S.-based companies found that higher levels of racial and gender diversity were associated with increased sales revenue, more customers, greater market share, and greater relative profits. Racial diversity, in particular, was one of the most important predictors of a company's competitive standing within its industry.

A study by the London Business School (2008) of 100 teams at 21 different companies found that work teams with equal numbers of women and men were more innovative and more productive than teams of any other composition. They attributed this finding to the fact that members on these teams were less likely to feel like "tokens" and better able to meaningfully contribute their ideas and efforts.

Using computer and mathematical modeling, (Page, 2007) has demonstrated that diverse teams consistently outperform even teams comprised only of the "highest-ability" agents.

Another more recent study of work teams (Woolley, et al., 2010) revealed that the intelligence level of individual team members was not a predictor of the collective intelligence of the team. However, one of the key predictors of the collective intelligence of a team was larger numbers of female team members.

Additional research has found benefits of gender diversity for start-up companies as well. For example, an analysis (Dow Jones VentureSource, 2011) of more than 20,000 venture-backed companies showed that successful start-ups have twice as many women in senior positions as unsuccessful companies. In addition, in a study of all investments made between 2000-2010 by U.S.-based venture capital (VC) firms (in U.S.-based companies), VC firms that invested in women-led businesses saw an improvement in their VC firm's performance (U.S. Small Business Administration, 2013).

In light of research studies such as these, technical organizations cannot afford to continue losing out on the benefits gender and other kinds of diversity can bring to technical advancements. Technology innovation is a creative process that involves teams. Often many teams, both large and small, work on a single product or service, from front-end requirements generation, through design and development, and product rollout and support. Clearly, it matters who sits at the table on these teams, and all of them would benefit from the increased participation of women.

However, as noted above, by and large, women are NOT participating in technology innovation roles, but rather, are found in the roles that support others who are engaging in leading-edge technology design and development. This point is not intended to be an evaluative statement about the importance of these support roles—indeed, they are critical. However, they are often not the roles leading to new technology breakthroughs. NCWIT partners with many of the world's largest companies and it is rare to find a woman, let alone a woman of color, leading any significant technical development effort. We need a diverse array of people contributing to both support and creation roles.

Only then will the technology we use every day be as rich and diverse as the people it serves.

Lucy Sanders, CEO
National Center for Women &
Information Technology (NCWIT)
and
Catherine Ashcroft
Senior Researcher National Center for Women &
Information Technology (NCWIT)

INTRODUCTION

Set a path in your mind with dreams and goals as signposts. Then let nothing deter you on your road to achievement and fulfillment.

I t seems like I've been advocating my whole professional life—25 years—for small, minority and women-owned businesses. The last 12 years have been spent specifically advocating for women in technology and historically underrepresented minorities who have been excluded from the tech boom.

I wholeheartedly subscribed to the mission of the nation's premier supplier diversity advocacy organizations and devoted much of my time, talent and resources over the years to increase the utilization and development of diverse suppliers nationally.

While others were focused on growing their businesses, I (alongside many other change agents in this space) felt compelled to participate in setting policy, providing guidance, direction and input on boards, councils, committees, and panels. My efforts were fueled by the ideal that supporting the full community would indeed be beneficial to me and my businesses as well.

It's apparent to me now, in looking back over my life, that I was born with the "servant gene." It's in my blood, part of my DNA, and has guided my actions since I was very young. I never minded pitching in or helping out whenever and wherever I was needed. In business, I consider myself to be a "Servant Leader" who diligently rolls up her sleeves to get the job done, motivating team members to do the same.

So, it should be no mystery that when confronted 11 years ago with the stark reality that women, African Americans and Hispanics were woefully underrepresented in the tech workforce and technology leadership positions in most companies, I was appalled. How could that be? Hadn't I been in tech pretty much all of my adult life? Am I not an African American woman? Don't I know many other people of color, male and female, running tech businesses?

The answer was a resounding 'Yes!'

However, when I was asked to join the Board of Directors of the National Center for Women & Information Technology (NCWIT) in 2005, I immediately went to work (again) to lend my time, talent and resources to this new organization, chartered by the National Science Foundation, in understanding what exactly was the problem we had to solve and why was it so important.

It has been an interesting journey, to be sure, and my intense support and advocacy has allowed me to develop and nurture an amazing network of other change agents across the country. It has also provided me the opportunity to meet some amazing leaders—presidents of the United States, senators, governors, CEOs of major corporations, African kings, and many other celebrities along the way.

I chose to write this book to chronicle my amazing journey, while shedding light on the challenges we face with the lack of diversity in today's tech workforce and its leadership.

It's not all bad news, as there is so much attention being paid to this problem. I truly believe there is a definite will to solving it. We absolutely have the resources to bring about change, and in this book, I will present some recommendations to meeting this challenge and pushing past it—breaking through to a new reality where everyone, even "a colored girl from Queens" has a chance to succeed in technology.

CHAPTER 1

UNCONSCIOUS OR NOT, BIAS IS ALIVE AND WELL!

Challenges exist to be overcome.

To be sure, I've seen my share of bias over the last three decades of running a tech company—and I know what it looks like. Bias has become more subtle of late, but it is alive and well. When it comes to the lack of diversity in tech, everyone is appropriately denouncing it and committing to fixing it, but the results speak for themselves.

The trouble is, women and underrepresented minorities (African Americans, Hispanics, and Native Americans) are not inventing the technology we all use every day. Nor are they being hired at U.S. corporations in proportion to their representation of the population—or, for that matter, their percent of the consumer base.

In fact, women hold only about 26 percent of all tech jobs in the U.S., despite the fact we occupy 57 percent of all professional jobs. When you break that

26 percent down by ethnicity, African American women hold 3 percent of all tech jobs and Latinas, just 1 percent. These numbers, provided by the U.S. Bureau of Labor Statistics are real—and in 2016, woeful!

When you look at the statistics for African American and Hispanic men, we find 5 percent of all U.S. tech jobs are held by Latinos and 4 percent are held by African American men. Therefore, to look at this situation from another perspective, almost three-quarters, or 74 percent, of all tech jobs in the U.S. are held by white and Asian males.

Why? Women comprise more than half of the U.S. population and Hispanics are the fastest growing ethnic group in the country. In fact, it is estimated that at the rate America is browning, we will have a majority minority population by 2050.

If these statistics were reversed, I wonder if we'd still be talking about this issue. I don't think so; I believe we would have fixed this lack of diversity a long time ago.

So why does this problem persist in one of the fastest growing and greatest wealth-producing industries in today's economy??

Well, for one, what is known as "unconscious bias" is being blamed for this nagging and persistent dilemma. Unconscious bias refers to a bias or leaning we are unaware of, and which happens outside of our control. It is a bias that happens automatically and is triggered by our brains making quick decisions based on our experiences, images we see, and other information we absorb every day.

So, following this train of thought, our brains tells us that technologists are predominantly white, geeky-looking men with poor people skills! Thus, if you don't fit that mold, the likelihood of your getting hired in tech is very remote.

To be sure, unconscious bias is real and does contribute to the problem. But, I'm here to tell you that not all bias is unconscious! We at NCWIT have been talking about and bringing attention to this issue since the early 2000s. We've been conducting research, developing training, producing resources and evidence-based best practices and the like, and yet, there has been very little movement of the numbers in the last dozen years. How long are we going to label the bias *unconscious*? I'm just saying ... where there's a will, there's a way. Do we really want to fix the problem or just continue to admire and caucus about it?

LEAVING THE TECH WORKFORCE
While the numbers have been slowing ticking up, another phenomenon has been occurring—women

are leaving the tech workforce 56 percent of the time. This means that as difficult as it is to attract women into tech jobs, by the time they reach mid-career, they leave the field.

Why? According to the Corporate Leavers Survey of the Level Playing Institute, two million people a year leave U.S. corporations due solely to perceived unconscious bias.

Where are they going? All too often, people assume women are leaving the workforce to start or care for a family. However, the numbers don't support that notion. Three out of four women who leave tech fields remain in the workforce; they are just leaving an unwelcoming or hostile work environment. They either leave tech for a business function in the same company, leave their current company for another, start their own business (as I did) or enter the public sector.

Regardless of why women are moving their careers out of tech, the turnover costs are real and the loss of corporate productivity and brain drain are significant. If done well, these are costs that can be averted. Three-quarters of the women in tech love what they do; however, that feeling of love won't stop them from leaving an environment that doesn't value their contribution enough to offer a place in which it is comfortable to work.

Some well-meaning companies, desirous of retaining women and people of color in their tech workforce, make the mistake of populating their development teams with just one diverse engineer. This is not a good idea, as that individual will undoubtedly feel isolated and alone in that setting—certainly not a strategy for success.

It's also not a good idea to depend on one underrepresented employee to be responsible for advancing a company's diversity goals. Executive management has to "own" diversity and make it a strategic imperative for the entire company, and someone has to be held accountable for meeting the objectives.

WHAT TO PUT IN THE WANT ADS

Other things to consider include discontinuing the use of a boilerplate "open for diversity" statement on want ads. According to researcher Aaron Kay, comments such as "women and minorities are encouraged to apply" only serve to decrease job appeal and anticipated "belongingness." Such wording typically cues potential candidates that diversity may be a "problem" or that the company is just looking for "demographically diverse" people to bring up their numbers.

Wording of want ads matters. It is critical to remove biased language such as: "We are looking for an aggressive, hard-driving, rock star" from job postings. This would be considered "gendered" language, and women would not even bother to apply.

WHAT'S IN THE PIPELINE?

Another very real cause of the lack of women and people of color in tech stems from an almost non-existent pipeline. It is imperative that we have systems in place to attract, educate and motivate all young people to the field of technology—especially since a vast majority of all 21st-century jobs require some form of technical aptitude. This is true of practically every industry, not just high tech. There are many industries, like automotive, financial services and pharmaceuticals, that are extremely dependent on technology to develop new products and run the business.

WHAT WE DO KNOW

Be that as it may, we are still not attracting enough girls and people of color into the tech field. This is a mystery that needs to be solved. We know that 8 out of 10 of the fastest growing jobs (or jobs in demand) are in the tech field. We know that tech is colorblind and gender-blind and the rate of invention has skyrocketed. We know that everything is made with code and tech jobs are paying above-average salaries. So why are we not attracting more diversity into the field?

Part of the problem is that tech is still a pretty well-kept secret. Young people have to be very intentional about seeking it out. I find it amazing that as of this writing, half of the high schools in the United States do not count computer science courses as either a math or science requirement for graduation. How can a course that is so critical to our country's future still be categorized as an elective? It just doesn't make sense. There's no incentive for a high-school student to choose to take an elective over a required course. None!

Experts agree that we have to increase the number of computer science degrees being conferred every year. Why? According to numbers compiled by the National Center for Women and IT (NCWIT) and Code.org, the U.S. will create 1 million more tech jobs by 2020 than we will have computer science graduates to fill them. *One million!*

How are we going to fill those jobs? What happens if we cannot? Where are the new workers going to come from if not from our schools? We've been importing a lot of talent from overseas instead of getting to the root of the problem and solving the basic needs here at home. Americans need to be trained to fill these jobs, especially women and people of color who have been consciously or unconsciously left out of the tech boom. You choose. It is my firm belief that we are still battling conscious bias in the workforce.

IT'S TIME TO PRESS THE RESET BUTTON!

According to *U.S. News & World Report*, jobs in computer science are growing at two times the national average. In some states, such as California, Connecticut, Delaware, New Jersey, and New York, computing jobs are growing at more than four times the state average. Still, 90 percent of schools nationwide don't offer computer science courses. *So unbelievable!*

At the same time, we know that student interest in computing is high. A recent report from Raytheon and the National Cyber Security Alliance found that about a quarter of young adults between 18 and 26 said they were interested in careers in cybersecurity, but nearly two-thirds (64 percent) said their high school didn't offer enough exposure to cybersecurity or computer science courses to pursue that interest.

Admittedly, this is not an easy fix, but are we doing enough to initiate a change? In this country, we have a shortage of teachers who possess the skills and resources to teach a computer science course. The rapid advancement of technology (and keeping courses fresh and relevant) can also pose significant problems for school districts with over-burdened budgets and an inability to keep pace with the changing times.

These problems, however, are not insurmountable. Pushing the reset button here would entail appropriating the funds and resources necessary to mount a major imperative to prepare educators to teach computer science in all U.S. high schools, develop the curriculum associated with these critical classes, and ensure they count as a math or science requirement for graduation.

By doing so, we would consciously begin to fix the pipeline part of this very real problem.

CHAPTER 2

THEN AND NOW

Go confidently in the direction of your dreams.

I t's amazing how quickly the world seems to be changing. Just look at how we've gone from only a precious few people important enough to have a mobile phone to what seems like EVERYONE on the planet chatting it up while walking down the street, riding on the train, dining in restaurants (and everywhere else). And, in only a few short years.

Or how about the extent to which the Internet has changed our lives? We do EVERYTHING online. From working, to bill paying, shopping, making reservations, travel, gaming, music, entertainment, and so much more. Not only can I now do anything I want from my computer, tablet and smartphone, I can even do these things from my car.

There has been an explosion of technological inventions, which has been so very exciting to witness. In fact, it is impossible to keep up with all the apps and entertainment available to us.

When I think back to my early days of selling the latest and greatest office automation tools to large and small businesses in New York City, I am amazed at how far tech has come as an industry. I excitedly sold the "first full-screen word processor" on the market—it took up an entire room! I also sold $10,000 electronic typewriters with a 1-line display. Yes, all you could see was one line of text at a time.

Or, how about the big, black, smoking fax machines we affectionately called Darth Vader that took three minutes a page to transmit. I couldn't get them to customers fast enough because the prior generation of fax machines used only thermal paper, was quite messy, and took six minutes to transmit a single page.

SO, WHO MAKES THE TECHNOLOGY?

Here's a question for you: Have you ever stopped to wonder just who is responsible for all the technological innovation over the last few years? Can you put a face on who will be inventing the technology of the future?

If I asked you to picture the computer scientist or genius of today who is behind all of the technology we've come to expect, what would that person look like?

I know—a youngish, nerdy-looking white guy with glasses, probably wearing a tee shirt and jeans (or hoodie), who would rather stick his finger into an electric pencil sharpener than engage you in conversation.

Am I right?

I know I am. And therein lies the problem. Why is that the image that comes to mind of almost everyone I ask? Who invented that image and why is it being perpetuated in the media and everywhere we look?

On the other hand, if I were to ask you who is consuming a great deal of this technology, would you know? Well, the answer is women—of all walks of life and especially women of color. They have every gadget, every tool, every app at their disposal. I know I do—and have become completely dependent on them.

But those women are not the ones who are inventing the cool devices and apps we are all using today. How different would the technology be if more women's perspectives, thought processes and experiences were built into these inventions?

I wonder if a woman had invented these things, would my smartphone or tablet work more effectively with my fingernails? *Just a thought!*

Many people out there are not convinced that we have a problem. The majority would stick their heads in the sand and say, "Well, as long as the technology is getting invented, who cares who's responsible for it?"

The problem is, my friends, that there aren't enough people in technology to meet our demands today. We also don't have enough people interested in pursuing computing as a discipline or a career. So who will be inventing the technology of the future? We just don't know, and therein lies the problem.

As I mentioned earlier, U.S. corporations will generate over one million net new computing jobs in the United States over the next few years, not positions being created by attrition or people leaving those tech jobs. Currently, only about one third of the people pursuing computing degrees could potentially fill those jobs. At the rate we are developing computer scientists in this country, more than half of those jobs could go unfilled.

This is a huge problem. Just ask any IT recruiter on college campuses across the country. The competition for those precious few college graduates is keen. We absolutely must find more individuals to fill those jobs.

So the question is, who is missing from the picture? The answer is—women and people of color.

Where are the women? Why are they not pursuing computing careers? Where are the African American and Latina women?

WHERE ARE THE WOMEN?

To answer this, we have to go back a few years to see where this problem began.

According to the U.S. Department of Labor Statistics, in the late 1980s and early 1990s, 37 percent of all technical occupations in the United States were held by women. Today, that number has dropped to 26 percent. African American and Latino men occupy approximately 9 percent of the technical occupations in U.S. corporations today, while African American and Latina women, 4 percent. (U.S. Dept of Labor Statistics, 2012 Current Population Survey)

Therefore, one problem is the fact that women and people of color are not participating in the development of technology.

Why the decline in the number of women occupying technical positions from just a few years ago? As I mentioned earlier, a study by NCWIT has found that 56 percent of women leave the discipline by the time they reach mid-career. That's twice the quit rate of men.

Couple that with the fact that fewer girls and young women are declaring computer science as a major discipline. This only adds to our problem.

To ensure that we have technology that's as broad and creative as the people it serves, the thoughts, ideas, and perspectives of women and people of color must be included.

Look at what happens when women are part of a team. Research has shown that there is little correlation between a group's collective intelligence and the IQs of its individual members. But if a group includes more women, its collective intelligence rises. ("Evidence for a Collective Intelligence Factor in the Performance of Human Groups," *Science,* October 2010, Woolley, Chabris, Pentland, Hashmi and Malone.)

Reaping the benefits of a broader pool of participants is not a new concept. We have countless examples in sports, business, politics, and other arenas. Imagine the possibilities of what technology could become if more women, Blacks, Hispanics, and Native Americans were active participants.

Still don't think we have a problem?

Well, as the CEO of a technology firm for more than three decades, I can tell you we do. As a social entrepreneur who is passionately committed to increasing the number of women and people of color in technology, I see firsthand that we do. As an active board member of the National Center for Women and IT (NCWIT) who regularly visits senior corporate IT and HR executives, I understand why we do. And, as an in-demand keynote speaker on Women and IT or "Unconscious Bias" all across this country and abroad, I soundly and consistently proclaim that we do.

The question is, what are we going to do about it? Oh, there's so much that can be done, and there is a lot that is being done. But we have so much more work to do.

BACK TO MY ROOTS

When I was first starting out in technology, I didn't realize that there was a dearth of women or people of color in the industry. I sold very early office technology on Wall Street. We had a good number of women on our team. In fact, my manager, Shirley, was African American. My branch manager, Felix, was African American. We worked very hard and were all very successful in our endeavors.

Let's be clear here. We were successful in *selling* technology. We were not *inventing* technology. There's a huge difference between the two.

After five very wonderful years selling technology for Exxon Office Systems Company in New York City, decision time came. Exxon was selling the division to another company, and I had to decide whether to stay with the new company—the buyer—go back into corporate Exxon or launch off on my own. I decided on the latter and became a first-time entrepreneur in January 1985.

Since I had found my love in technology sales, it seemed reasonable to want to stay in the industry. It was what I knew then and what I loved. I felt Exxon had trained me well and that I could make it on my own.

My first company began by continuing to support the customers who had made an investment in Exxon equipment. That support included training new operators, replacement staffing for that type of equipment, and overflow word processing work.

My initial customers were household names— AT&T, Exxon, the New York Times, and Hoffman LaRoche. My company supported all of these firms over the first 3 to 5 years of our existence, and experienced consistent growth as a result.

However, as is the case with technology, the Exxon equipment began to be refreshed and replaced with new, state-of-the-art equipment from other companies. You see, Exxon was no longer in the tech business and customers had to look elsewhere for equipment to service their needs.

To stay relevant, we had to regularly reengineer, reinvent, and identify new customers on an ongoing basis. As you can imagine, technology never sits down and stays still. It is constantly advancing—and to be in this industry, you have to do so as well.

I always had the perspective of looking to service customers from the vantage point of the user. There was a constant search to see how we could make users' jobs easier, deliver more automation, and show them how to best embrace technology for better results.

For that reason, we have remained predominantly a services organization, as opposed to a product-driven one. I knew that service was the key differentiator of IT firms on the market, and felt that those who could best support their customers and continuously add value, would be the ones who could sustain themselves over time.

However, had I been more focused on innovation back in the 1980s or '90s, imagine how I could have participated and contributed to all of the new technology that abounds today. I have seen unimaginable advancements in how we work, play, and live our very lives as a result of new technology.

Just think, when I was selling early fax technology back in the 1980s, when one page took six minutes to transmit, no one imagined that we could achieve the same results in a matter of seconds. And that we could do so without having to print out a document, place the telephone receiver in a coupler or another device, and wait for it to finish.

And that awful thermal paper, ugh!!! So glad that went the way of the dinosaur.

As an early user of office technology, there were many things that, if I think back, I could have improved upon had I had the notion. But that was not my focus. I was intent on selling as many of those devices as fast as I could.

Staying focused on my objectives clearly worked well for me. I learned the art of the sale very well, and soon came to discover that the product I was selling didn't matter. I could sell technology, ideas, desired states, or any other tangible product or intangible concept. As long as the customer per-ceived value from my recommendations, I was able to close the sale.

Back then, we didn't know (or care) who created the technology we were selling. At least today, we can put faces next to some products—Bill Gates, Mark Zuckerberg, Steve Jobs—you get the picture.

Unfortunately, there are no women's names associated with innovation that are as widely known as the three gentlemen I just mentioned.

And therein lies the problem.

WHERE ARE THE WOMEN?

Why are we not inventing technology? We are smart. We are creative. We are innovative. We are hardworking and deeply concerned about the state of this world. So, I ask again, *where are the women inventing technology?*

Information technology informs all aspects of modern society. Including women and people of color is so very important to the future of technology. When we bring a wider variety of people into technology, our innovation will be enhanced through the invaluable contributions brought in by diverse perspectives.

We also know that diversity promotes equality. Because of the increasingly crucial role technology plays in all of our lives, being more inclusive and involving people from different backgrounds in the creation of technology, can help to break down and eradicate gender and racial economic inequalities.

WHO WILL FILL THE JOBS?

I will say this again. 1.4 million net new computing-related jobs will be added to the U.S. labor rolls by 2018. That's an increase of 22 percent from 2008. These computing jobs are high-paying and often times can be done from remote locations—like home—and have flexible hours associated with them.

However, the number of people graduating from college with computer or information sciences degrees has been steadily decreasing since 2004. At this rate, fewer than one third of the vacant computing jobs expected by 2018 could potentially be filled. In addition, many non-IT jobs today require deep knowledge of computing as well.

How are we going to fill these jobs if we're not working hard on filling the pipeline with the workforce of tomorrow? That workforce is increasingly women and people of color. Yes, the same ones who are missing, in large part, from the technical workforce of today.

The computing industry is such a good career choice for women. In June of 2009, when the overall unemployment rate in the U.S. was 9.7 percent, the unemployment rate for computer and math occupations was 5.4 percent, and for women in these fields, it was only 3.8 percent (Bureau of Labor Statistics).

This relative stability in IT is expected to continue, not decline. In fact, computing-related occupations are still projected to be the fastest-growing segment of the professional workforce between now and 2018. In fact, computing-related occupations are projected to grow by 22 percent and add more jobs than any other category of professional occupation.

CLOSING THE WAGE GAP WITH TECH

According to U. S. Census data, women generally still make less money than men. (Another problem that needs fixing.) While in years past, women typically earned about $.78 to every dollar a man earned, women in computing-related occupations were better off. Their median income was 86 percent of men's earnings.

Despite all of the good data that exists today about IT and computing being an excellent career choice for women, the myths still abound. These myths are causing parents and school counselors to steer their children away from computing.

We can all help dispel prevailing negative myths about the IT industry by simply sharing the facts. Low unemployment, high profitability, and a society that is increasingly IT-dependent, means that computing is an excellent career choice for girls, women, and people of color.

With that said, how are we preparing our children with skills for the 21st century? The answer: Not very well. Please read on.

CHAPTER 3

EDUCATION IS THE KEY

*Face every day with determination
and the firm belief that achieving your dream
is not just a possibility, but your destiny.*

Would it surprise you to know that most high schools don't teach computer science—not even the basics? It should, especially given the fact mentioned earlier that there will be over 1 million more U.S. jobs in the tech sector in the next decade than computer science graduates to fill them, according to Code.org, a nonprofit launched in 2013 to promote computer science in schools.

Failure to teach students basic theory behind how computer technology works has several implications—none of them positive. First, employers are clamoring for qualified people to fill tech-related jobs. Yet students aren't introduced to this potentially high-paying field as they take the first steps toward a career.

This is particularly true for women and people of color, two groups woefully underrepresented in technology jobs. Earlier exposure to computer science careers not only points more people toward the industry, it also eases stereotypes about who "belongs" in these jobs.

Basic education in computer science makes sense for all students—even kids who'll never earn a living writing software code.

A few years ago, schools in Estonia, one of the European Baltic states and a global leader in science and technology education, began teaching kids as young as age 7 to write computer code. The idea wasn't to create an army of app developers; it was to help citizens develop smarter relationships with technology, computers and the Web.

In 2012, *Time* magazine reported that the only serious computing class available to most students is AP computer science, which focuses on Java programming. And even that course was offered at just 10 percent of American high schools.

Code.org says that 33 of 50 states don't offer graduation credit for computer science courses. Where courses are offered, they're usually electives, which don't fulfill core math or science requirements and discourage bright college-bound students from taking them.

I know I've never been a school administrator, but it is clear to me that computer science should absolutely be taught in every school in the country. Secondly, taking such classes must be required to graduate.

SWIMMING TO GRADUATE

When I was growing up in New York City, I had to pass a swimming test in order to graduate from high school. I guess school officials felt that although we were in the middle of the borough of Queens with no water in sight, knowing how to swim might just one day be important to us. So important, that we could not graduate from high school without showing an aptitude in the pool.

Well, as it turns out, floundering around enough to pass that test did not instill a love of swimming in my heart. However, years later, after taking a series of swimming courses at the local YMCA in Newark, New Jersey, my love of swimming did blossom, and it is a great source of exercise for me today. In fact, this comfort in deep water allowed me to confidently learn how to scuba dive and become certified with my husband back in 2000 on the island of Bonaire.

Other than that experience, swimming has not made one bit of difference in my professional life, and probably never will. On the other hand, my learning how to type in high school, which was not a condition of graduation, has afforded me the ability to be successful in every job or project in which I've ever been involved. That was a life-changing skill. I can only imagine how different my life might have been had I learned how to code back then.

THE "ASPIRATIONS IN COMPUTING" AWARD —AND BEYOND

I am seeing the difference computer science is having on high school girls who apply for NCWIT's "Aspirations in Computing" award. Since 2007, about 4,700 girls have been recognized regionally and nationally for their demonstrated aptitude and leadership in technology.

These young women demonstrate clearly what a focus on computer science education can produce. They are smart, beautiful, active, creative, driven and already successful. They speak multiple languages, dance, sing, play sports, write books and start their own companies—all while still excelling in other high school subjects.

The Aspirations winners I meet around the country are all successful and know where they are headed. The future is much brighter knowing these young women will make a difference in this world. I am so committed to this program and am working hard to multiply the effects of it many fold.

A few years ago, the NCWIT Aspire IT program was created to reach into middle schools to bring about an awareness of computing and instill a love of technology at an even younger age. The high school Aspirations girls are enabled by funding, sponsorship and guidance from NCWIT members to conduct after-school or summer camp programs to help the younger girls learn computing.

This, too, has become a highly successful program, changing lives at a very young age.

Other programs changing young lives include Black Girls Code (www.blackgirlscode.com) founded by Kimberly Bryant in 2010, and Girls Who Code, (www.girlswhocode.com) founded by Reshma Saujani in 2012. Both these program founders are dynamic change agents, committed to impacting girls' lives one at a time.

CHAPTER 4

A PEEK BEHIND DOOR #4

Face every day with determination and the firm belief that achieving your dream is not just a possibility, but your destiny.

Also missing from the ranks today are senior female IT leaders. This is mainly because there aren't enough women entering the field or staying long enough to break through to the levels of senior executive. Women tend to hire and mentor other women, paying close attention to bringing others along with them. This dynamic is critical to increasing the overall numbers.

I look at the example of Ann Mulcahy, former CEO of Xerox Corporation. She mentored and groomed Ursula Burns for years to prepare her to eventually assume the role of CEO upon Mulcahy's retirement. To this day, Ursula is still the only African American female CEO of a major U.S. technology company. We need more examples of this type of leadership development if we are to be successful in bridging the leadership gap.

I had the pleasure of meeting Ursula Burns a couple of years ago at the Black Enterprise Women of Power Summit. She is so accomplished and so very impressive. She exudes power and personality. I've admired her from afar for many years. She is certainly an excellent role model for me and countless others.

But for how long will she be the only one?

THE WORKPLACE NEEDS ETHNICALLY DIVERSE WOMEN LEADERS

Ethnically diverse women leaders are sorely needed in the workplace. Not only do they possess the skills and aptitudes found in most women, they also bring a rich cultural diversity to the workplace that lends itself to more inclusion and to fostering a more welcoming environment.

Thinking back to my first manager in a technology setting, Shirley taught me so much more than just how to be a successful salesperson. She was also concerned about my wardrobe and making sure I was always well put-together. From my suits, silk blouses and ties, to my first strand of real pearls, Shirley was my chief counsel and confidante in those matters. My pearls were bought from her own collection at a price I could afford back then.

Shirley invested in me her time, interest and talent to single-handedly ensure my success, and I will forever be grateful to her for doing so.

My 18-inch double strand of pearls from her collection is still one of my most prized possessions. It's amazing when I think how long I've had them—at least 35 years, and they are still classic and elegant.

Not only did Shirley play an integral role in my life and early career, so did Felix, my branch manager. As I mentioned earlier, Felix was also African American, but at Exxon, even back then, it just wasn't that unusual to see African Americans in leadership positions.

While still in corporate Exxon before going with the office systems division, my first Department Head of Administrative Services was Bertha Augburn, another African American female. I remember feeling so proud of her. What an incredible role model she set for me as a very young woman just starting her career.

Bertha taught me a lot and became a lifelong friend. When I moved to New Jersey from New York, I reconnected with Bertha at church. How thrilled I was to find her again. We quickly regained our friendship, which remained strong until her untimely death in 2006. To this day, whenever I go visit another family friend, Marcy, who lives right around the corner from Bertha's house, I cannot help but glance at what used to be her front door, wishing I could see her opening it and welcoming me in again as she had done so many times before.

FELIX BELIEVED IN ME

Back to Felix. He too made an unforgettable investment in me. You see, I had been strongly encouraged by several people to pursue the sales career path in Exxon's newly created division, Exxon Office Systems Company. I had never been exposed to sales before, but others saw characteristics in me they felt would translate into sales success: friendliness, love of talking, love of people, great vocabulary, and dedication to excellence. So, I took the "aptitude test" Exxon was using at the time that would magically determine my penchant to succeed in sales.

I scored low in the empathy portion of the test. Really??? Were they kidding me? How do you measure empathy?

I was one of six kids growing up in New York City (with very little personal physical space). Add to the household my two parents and a dog or two, and you've got one full home—sometimes with only one bathroom. How could I score low on empathy?

In my mind I was thinking, *What exactly is empathy, and what does it have to do with sales?* I knew the technical definition of the word, but was lost on the application of it in this context.

What I came to understand was that empathy is the characteristic that allows you to put yourself in another person's shoes. To be successful in sales, you had to possess the ability to do just that. At least, that's what the test's answer guide insisted. And according to protocol, I should have been passed over for a sales position.

Well, Felix sat me down in his midtown Manhattan branch manager's office and told me he was going to take a chance on me despite what the test results showed. He thought I could overcome that one deficiency and have a successful sales career. I was so grateful to him that I made up my mind that very day—there was no way I was going to let him down or make him regret his decision. I was determined to work harder than anyone else to prove him right.

It worked! I was named Rookie of the Year for NY Midtown my first year, over-achieved quota and was promoted every year throughout my tenure with Exxon Office Systems Company.

So much for standardized tests and the barriers to entry they can present. (Again, a societal problem that needs addressing.)

I wonder who else would have made those decisions and investments in a young African American woman in the early 1980s?

MENTORS WHO LOOK LIKE ME

What I do know is that it is important for people of color to see and be motivated by others of their race in positions of leadership. For me, it invoked a strong sense of pride and commitment to be the best I could be for them to also be proud of me. I didn't want to let any of them down.

Who knows where I'd be today had it not been for Bertha, Felix and Shirley?

With their years of support, I had enough courage to launch my first business in 1985 as a result of what I had gained from my association with them. Exxon Office Systems was sold to Harris Corporation at the end of 1984, and for the first time in my life, I was no longer working for Exxon Corporation.

I could have gone back inside corporate Exxon— but after having been in field sales for five years, selling state-of-the-art technology on Wall Street and living an exciting life of meeting new people every day and servicing my customers, I just didn't see a corporate staff position as very exciting or inspiring. However, I knew that if I needed to, I could always go back and be unequivocally welcomed.

Nor was I interested in going to work for any of the companies I considered "the competition." I had never worked for any company other than Exxon, and felt a responsibility and kinship to the firm.

In my mind, what made the most sense was to take the next logical step in my career and start my own business. In January of 2017, I will celebrate 32 years as a technology business owner. Who knew?

THREE DECADES OF TECH SUCCESS

It is difficult to even imagine how things have worked out over the past 30 years. Through the good times and bad, I persisted and trusted in God. The time has literally flown. I wish more women could experience the joys of tech entrepreneurship. It has been such a totally fulfilling experience, one that I have truly enjoyed and never regretted.

* * * * *

WHO'S MISSING?

Who else is missing from the equation today? It's time to look behind Door #4 for a healthy pipeline of young talent. It is so critical to introduce girls—and boys of color—to technology at a very young age and keep them engaged as they grow older. This should be easier to do today than when I was growing up.

Many children have access to computing almost at birth. They grow up with electronics as toys and learning aids, with multiple computers in the home and at school, smartphones, smart televisions, and increasingly smart homes in which they live and smart cars in which they ride.

So, technology is not a new concept for them; they are growing up to be technology consumers. What we need to do is build their awareness and desire to become technology creators.

By no means is this access to technology evenly spread across regions, socio-economic strata or racial boundaries. We still have far too many young girls and boys of color in this country who do not have access to technology at all; hundreds of others do not have adequate access.

For example, there may be only one computer in the nursery school, pre-K or kindergarten class. By middle school, access to technology needs to be very pervasive so that by the time children reach high school, they have a 1:1 ratio of students to computers.

But, of course, this is not the reality. I've already shared the startling statistic that less than 10 percent of all high schools in the United States offer courses in computer science. Far fewer require computer science as a requirement for graduation.

No wonder we have a tech worker shortage!!

We must begin to educate our young people in computer science at an earlier age to begin to build the healthy, robust pipeline of future workers the American economy needs today and will increasingly need in the future.

It's time to break down Door #4 and open the floodgates to the hidden geniuses in so many urban centers and rural communities across this great land.

CHAPTER 5

BREAK EVERY PANE!

*Be strong. Be brave. Above all, remain
committed to your dreams, your goals,
and most importantly, yourself.*

Most corporate cultures have developed over a very long time. Since they were original-ly developed by men for men, a masculine culture continues to permeate most organizations. Also, 97 percent of all U.S. corporations are still male -led. There is usually a small percentage of directors or senior management that is either female or people of color. Consequently, very little has changed over the years.

This has resulted in unconscious bias being prevalent in the workplace, often making it unwel-coming to women and people from different cultures. These biases, which stem from homogeneous envi-ronments, however unintentional, can cause others to feel like outsiders, like they don't belong or not wanted.

I never felt that way when I worked for Exxon. I felt at ease in every position I held; each supervisor treated me like a valued contributor. Even in the beginning when I worked as a secretary or word processor, I felt that I belonged and was valued.

This sense of well-being could have been attributed to the fact that I was young and just happy to be there. Or given the fact that I had never worked for any other company, I simply had no basis for comparison. Looking back, even with the knowledge I now possess of unconscious bias in the workplace, my opinion doesn't change.

I also believe my strong sense of self-confidence contributed to my level of comfort in every setting in which I worked—seven or eight different departments and locations over 11 years. The first three were internships while I was still in college. After that, I was promoted every 18 to 24 months before landing at Exxon Office Systems Company in 1980, a new division created to enable Exxon to enter the very profitable and influential office technology industry.

BEING PREPARED WAS KEY

I always felt I was well prepared to fill the administrative roles I was assigned; I could type 80 words per minute and take dictation at 120 words per minute. These and other business skills I honed and perfected while still in high school. My love of reading from a very young age equipped me with a broad view and an expansive vocabulary.

My siblings and I still laugh about how I would disappear for hours and hide in the closet, under the bed, or wherever I could find a little peace and quiet to read my books. With both parents and five siblings, being successful in finding a quiet reading spot in our small NYC apartments or suburban homes was not an easy task. Every week, I would visit the library, leave with an armful of books and race home to read all of them, repeating the process once the last book was finished.

I didn't want to watch cartoons or play house; I wanted to be left alone, and I wanted to read!! They all thought I was very strange...

You see, we were a typical working-class southern family who had migrated to the Big City in search of better job opportunities for my father. When I was one year old, he moved us from Augusta, Georgia— my city of birth—to the Bronx and got a job as a superintendent of an apartment building.

There were only 3 of us at that time—my sister, Karen, my brother, Darrell and myself. My three younger sisters—Ondria, April and Mira—were all born in New York City. We moved a lot early on because each new job my father secured as a building superintendent meant we had to live in the building he serviced.

During those early years, my father enrolled in school, earning several degrees while continuing to be the breadwinner of his very large family. Later, he was employed as a Division Manager by the NYC Board of Education until his retirement.

We didn't travel much (except for the annual drive down to Augusta, GA and Greenville, SC—my parents' respective hometowns—to visit the grandparents). We didn't go on spring break, summer vacations, cruises or any other such thing common for young people today. Consequently, my escape was in the books I devoured. What I didn't realize at the time was how my love of reading was preparing me for the life I was destined to live.

So, at Exxon, I was a happy girl. I had purpose. I belonged.

TODAY'S WORK ENVIRONMENTS

Today's work environments, especially in the tech departments, are so very much male-dominated, that it is common for institutional barriers for women to exist. This is borne out in the hiring companies do from referrals. With regard to referrals, people tend to recommend people much like themselves, a phenomenon known as "assortative matching."

According to a study for the Federal Reserve Bank of New York, 64 percent of employees recommended candidates of the same gender, while 71 percent referred candidates of the same race or ethnicity.

At least one study has found that women re ferred for entry-level tech jobs are significantly more likely to be hired than women without referrals. The same study found that for executive high-tech jobs, referred candidates are much more likely to be men than women.

To break that cycle, it is important for recruiting managers to expand their normal base of networks or campuses and recruit in diverse networks. In other words, they need to break every pane of glass to discover the wealth of untapped talent that exists out there.

WHERE CAN WE FIND GREAT CANDIDATES?

Historically Black colleges and universities (HBCUs) and Minority Serving Institutions (MSIs) are great resources for women and people of color. In addition, there are national organizations like the Black Data Processing Association (BDPA) with chapters all over the country. Networking with BDPA and similar organizations like the Society of Women Engineers (SWE) can also yield great candidates.

Go to where the women are—Women2.0, Linux Chicks, NCWIT Aspirations Community, WITI and other groups are ripe sources of excellent technical talent.

Another often-overlooked ready resource of candidates is community colleges. Sometimes, this is the only option available to low-opportunity youth to attend college. It was for me. I am a proud graduate of LaGuardia Community College (named for former NYC mayor, Fiorello LaGuardia). There was no money for college when I was growing up, so community college was my only way to go. And, it is still the only way for many deserving underprivileged youth today.

As was the case for me, once community college graduates enter the workplace, they can continue their education with the benefit of tuition reimbursement.

There are scores of competent, intelligent, hard-working future employees studying at community colleges all across the country. It should definitely be part of a recruiting manager's strategy when seeking to identify and recruit qualified, diverse candidates.

Every pane of glass shielding the different faces of technical talent must be shattered to reveal who's behind it and remove the barriers to entry for diverse candidates.

SCHEMAS—SELECTIVE DISCERNMENT

Again, another phenomenon impacting women in the workplace today is unconscious bias. Unconscious bias results from what are known as "schemas." Schemas are like shortcuts, necessary to live, and everyone has them. We need schemas to make sense of information and to function in this world. They let us pay attention to only select information. But they can also cause us to miss or misinterpret certain things, leading to unconscious bias.

Here's a test. Who is the computer scientist in this photo?

Did you guess the young, white, nerdy-looking male? Of course you did! Society has told us over and over again that's what computer scientists look like. You didn't need to look it up or do any research; you relied on a built-in schema to get to a quick answer. And, that happens every day in a multitude of ways.

Want more proof? How often have you assumed the one woman at a meeting was the administrative assistant—there to take minutes and fetch coffee (or take the lunch order)? Or, how often is a female associate not copied on a technical email?

Society is definitely biased about gender and technology. A snapshot of a study done by Project Implicit solicits an automatic response to the relationship between gender and science.

Percent of web respondents with each score

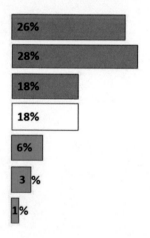

Strong automatic association of Male with Science and Female with Liberal Arts	26%
Moderate automatic association of Male with Science and Female with Liberal Arts	28%
Slight automatic association of Male with Science and Female with Liberal Arts	18%
Little to no automatic preference between gender and academic domains	18%
Slight automatic association of Male with Liberal Arts and Female with Science	6%
Moderate automatic association of Male with Liberal Arts and Female with Science	3%
Strong automatic association of Male with Liberal Arts and Female with Science	1%

In this study, 78 percent of study respondents automatically associated science with men and liberal arts with women (the top 3 shaded boxes above). Only 10 percent associated women with science and men with liberal arts. With this type of response, is it any wonder we have such a science and technology gender gap?

By the way, this was a national study of both men and women. Men aren't the only ones who are biased; women are as well.

You can determine your own level of bias by visiting www.projectimplicit.com and taking the test.

Knowledge is indeed power. The only way we will be able to reverse the bias rampant in corporations today is to understand where we each stand as individuals and be accountable for our own actions.

Another example of unconscious bias was borne out by the Columbia Business School study, known as the "Roizen case study." Frank Flynn, Associate Professor at Columbia Business School, who shared the following:

> *Before class, we had one section of students read the original case and the other section read a version of the case called "Howard Roizen." Nothing was changed in the Howard version except for all the relevant pronouns. The students then went online*

and rated Heidi/Howard on several dimen-
sions. The results were disturbing, as you
might imagine. Students were incredibly
harsh when they thought "Roizen" was a
woman, but not when they thought Roizen
was a man. Most of these differences are
highly significant.

Three questions were asked of the male and female Columbia Business School students about "Roizen," with startling results. Both men and women students participated in this study and both rated Roizen higher when they thought he was male. I'm pretty sure none of those students would have classified themselves as biased. However, the outcomes paint a different picture. It's what makes this such a difficult problem to overcome—the bias, in some cases, is a natural, automatic response. Be that as it may, not all bias is unconscious.

HOW CAN SOCIETAL BIAS BE OFFSET?

What can we do to offset or counterattack societal bias? Well, we know that bias is much more prevalent in homogenous environments where everyone is pretty much the same (think white males). So, when someone from a different culture or gender joins the group, the norms of the homogeneous group can or may be offputting to the newcomer, who has a different set of experiences and norms.

The value derived from cultural and gender diversity is lacking in homogenous environments. Every effort should be made to consciously introduce diversity into all groups—and with more than just one "token" individual.

Some companies today have really begun to not only value diversity, but also demand it. Hiring managers increasingly will not accept a slate of candidates to fill their open positions unless it is a diverse representation. Similarly, companies have begun to voice displeasure when sales teams consisting of all white males show up for presentations or meetings. I know of some organizations that have made it quite clear that only diverse teams will be acceptable at future meetings.

Why? It is because they recognize that the solution being offered by a homogenous group of individuals will not be as rich and valuable as one from a diverse group.

That's breaking a glass pane, for sure! It's also important that the presenting team be able to interact comfortably with the diverse team sourcing the products or services.

WHAT ABOUT WOMEN AND BIAS?

We know that in the case of women, the harmful effects of unconscious bias in the workplace tend to lead women to these outcomes. They:

- Don't speak up in meetings
- Are reluctant to take leadership positions
- Are overly harsh about their own work
- Sometimes discount their own performance

Eventually, women will leave a hostile work environment where they don't feel welcomed or valued. That's detrimental to every organization that invests millions in their recruiting and training activities. So, it's important to note that the lack of diversity definitely impacts the bottom line of corporations every day.

Diversity and inclusion have to be more than just words. As a female and/or person of color, be public about your needs and expectations. Senior leadership is critical to effectively building your brand as an inclusive, welcoming place to work.

In regard to business processes, bias here will also make women leave, even if hiring managers have managed to hire them. Are women in some of the top technical jobs in your organization? Or are they in the "empathy" jobs? Can they see themselves aspiring to secure a CIO or CTO position? If senior leadership and all his direct reports look exactly the same—white males—the answer is no.

REVAMPING THE PERFORMANCE APPRAISAL

Performance appraisals offer another glass pane in need of breaking. Women are often evaluated on luck and collaboration, men on skill. We saw that very clearly in the Roizen case study from Columbia Business School. The very same person, when thought to be female, was evaluated more harshly than when considered to be male. Performance appraisals should be audited by social scientists to ensure they are gender friendly.

In addition, audit all job postings for unintentionally biased or gendered language. The wording might be the very reason diverse candidates are not applying for open positions.

WHAT DOES THE WORKPLACE LOOK LIKE?

Physical environment counts a lot. Research has shown that women are less likely to be attracted to computing majors and anticipate less success in these fields when asked about their interests while sitting in a room with *Star Wars* posters, stacked soda cans, action figures, and other stereotypical "geek" objects.

(Cheryan, S., Plaut, V., Davies, P., & Steele, C. (2009). Ambient belonging: How stereotypical cues impact gender participation in computer science. *Journal of Personality and Social Psychology*, 97(6), 1045-1060)

HOW DOES YOUR ORGANIZATION REALLY VALUE DIVERSITY?

It is so important to not only communicate, but to demonstrate that your company values diversity in its workforce. Below is a pane of glass in serious need of breaking.

Strong, committed and visible support from senior leadership is a critical component to changing an organization's culture. It doesn't really matter what type of change is envisioned. Without a visible leadership effort, any initiative will fall short of its desired goals.

I know this to be true from my many years serving in leadership positions in supplier diversity. Both the National Minority Supplier Development Council (NMSDC) and the Women's Business Enterprise National Council (WBENC) provide guidance to corporations desirous of diversifying their supply chain with minority and women-owned companies. The number one component for success has always been a written commitment statement from the CEO. Companies that miss this critical first step will never achieve the level of success they desire.

BEST PRACTICES IN SUPPLIER DIVERSITY

For over 15 years, I served on the NMSDC National Corporation of the Year Committee and spent endless hours reviewing thousands of applications from companies eager to be named the best company for supplier diversity each year.

They had to include their CEO Commitment Statement as part of their submission. Equally important, the CEO had to sign the application. Failure to do so resulted in immediate disqualification and elimination from the process. That's how critically we viewed strong leadership.

Another best practice for increasing the number of diverse suppliers was to set goals and objectives, then hold people accountable for achieving them. As we all have heard, what gets measured, gets done.

When you empower and provide incentives to change agents within an organization, things also get done. For best results, tie performance to compensation. That's when you'll really see change begin to materialize. The floors will be littered with broken glass!

You also want to market the fact that you are actively seeking women and diverse candidates to add to your technical ranks. Expand your marketing efforts in the diverse media markets and channels. Join and network with the organizations that cater to diverse populations. Attend conferences and annual summits like NCWIT and the Grace Hopper Celebration. The latter event was created by the Anita Borg Institute as a means of bringing corporations together with technical women. Stream your jobs on the NCWIT site, and support organizations that are working to fix the problem.

Breaking every pane that holds back women and people of color from participating at the highest levels of technology should be an imperative of every U.S. corporation. It's not just a problem for the government and non-profit sector to address. Without broader corporate support, we will still be shaking our heads and wringing our hands 20 years from now.

Is that the legacy we want to leave?

CHAPTER 6

KEEP YOUR EYES ON THE PRIZE

We need not wait to see what others do.

F aster ... Better ... Cheaper ... has been the rallying cry in business for many years. Remaining status quo for any organization is a death knell. The global marketplace is insatiable when it comes to the "next big thing." Tech companies are competing hard to be the first to market with "it" and a lot of money is being invested in research and development of new technology. At the same time, tons of dollars are being spent on litigation over patent infringements; this is not a game! Innovation is key; reengineering is a must; feeding the tech frenzy is Job Number One!

Look how far we've come in technology advancements in my career alone:

- In high school, I learned to type on an IBM Selectric typewriter (I still own one and it works just fine.)
- In college, I used magnetic card machines

- At Exxon, I became an expert Vydec Operator (the first full-screen word processor on the market)
- In midtown and lower Manhattan, I sold these firsts:
    - $10,000 electronic typewriters with 1-line display
    - First-generation facsimile machines that took 6 minutes to send/receive a page (you had to put the telephone handset in a coupler to get the signal and the image was transferred onto thermal paper as it spun around in a separate housing)
    - Information processors (predecessor of the PC)

I know, I know, this all sounds like a lesson in ancient history rather than experiences of a single career. When I share my story with high school or college students, it sounds unreal to them, and certainly nothing they can even grasp. But, in the 1970s and '80s, these devices were the cutting-edge market leaders.

As much as we think we got it going on with today's smart devices and wearables, we'll again look back in 20 years and see just how far we've come. We'll wonder how we even existed with the smartphones of today compared to what we'll be using then.

Question: When was the last time you used a stand-alone fax machine? Or a beeper? A pay phone? I rest my case ...

It is this constant quest for innovation that drives most companies these days. However, innovation is not just something you can open a can or Ziploc bag to access—it comes from the brilliant minds of designers, architects and developers. The more diverse the base of people designing new technology, the broader and more far-reaching the resulting products will be.

Since designers and inventors bring their different experiences to their work, it's inevitable they will approach a problem from different perspectives. That, in turn, will lead to different solutions, resulting in technology as broad and diverse as the population it serves. That's what leads to innovation.

Conversely, not tapping into a diverse talent pool limits the design potential. The same type of people designing technology won't necessarily push boundaries or stretch limits. They don't know what they don't know! They share similar experiences.

As I've mentioned, including women in work teams raises the collective intelligence of the group. Additionally, the most cited (and consequently, the most effective) technology patents are those created by cross-gender teams.

One thing is clear ... innovation is much too important to leave to chance.

Over the years, I have witnessed time and again the genius of a diverse team. Whether I had five employees or 75, my employee base has always been diverse. I have always been committed to the value of diversity. There was room for everyone's ideas, questions and input on my work teams.

I have never run a company in which I made all the decisions or even came up with the best ideas. I like the team approach to business and employ the same approach to life itself. It certainly "took a village" to raise children in New York City and New Jersey when mine were growing up, and it definitely took a broad team of advisors, lenders, investors, employees, partners and family to grow a successful business.

Today, it still takes a team to take care of me. I can't do it all. I've stopped trying. As I share with audiences all the time, I push back the notion of work-life balance. Personally, I don't think such a thing exists. Rather, I strive for work-life integration and believe in outsourcing—whether that's housework or cooking or you name it. There's someone out there who enjoys and makes a living doing such tasks. I choose to avail myself of those services as opposed to trying to do it all myself.

ALIGNING WITH DIVERSE CULTURES
AROUND THE WORLD

Most companies today, large and small, are competing in the global marketplace. This requires a diverse marketing strategy. What works for the U.S. will not work in many other parts of the world. Language, culture and societal norms all come into play when penetrating new geographic markets. To be successful, it is critically important to align with people native to targeted regions of interest.

Employing ethnically diverse individuals who speak the language and understand the culture of the region yields tremendous value to any global endeavor.

The same is true in technology. Employing women and people of diverse backgrounds who understand the varying market segments, and possess an affinity for what resonates with them, is of tremendous value. Unfortunately, however, the tech sector is still a mostly white, male-dominated society. Too bad, because to quote Jesse Jackson, "We don't know how good technology can really be until everyone can participate." We saw this idea manifest in other white, male-dominated activities like baseball, golf, tennis, politics, and other fields.

DIVERSITY DATA DISCLOSURES

Recently, some of the leading tech firms in the country disclosed the demographic information of their employee base. The firms included Intel, Google, and Apple. About 40 companies in all took the courageous step of opening their kimonos and showing us what we already knew.

While the percentage of women and people of color is woefully low (one could argue non-existent), I thought that their decision to abandon the acquisition of legal protection and disclose the data was a huge, positive first step in recognizing they have a problem, in understanding its potential impact, and ultimately, in working hard to solve their problem.

Through NCWIT, there is tremendous support and resources available to help companies take the necessary steps to understand their culture and determine what can be done to make theirs a more welcoming and inclusive environment.

All too often, we hear that firms cannot locate qualified, diverse talent. My response to that statement is, "Where are you looking?" The same old recruiting strategy you've used for years will not produce different results. (We know the definition of thinking it will, right?)

Once again, my advice to recruiters is to spend more time at Historically Black Colleges and Universities (HBCUs) and other Minority Serving Institutions (MSIs) as a source for untapped talent. A majority of women are enrolled at these schools. Likewise, community colleges provide another great source of talented women and minorities.

While there wasn't money for me to go away to college when I was young, and that may still hold true in many homes today, it does not lessen the will or determination to succeed. I am a proud community college graduate, and grateful that Exxon Corporation had the foresight and methodology to grow and develop young talent like myself. If this strategy could work 40 years ago, surely it can work today.

TACKLING SOCIAL ILLS WITH TECHNOLOGY JOBS

In fact, I believe that by attracting and training/ developing talent from diverse communities, we can solve several great ills of our time—unemployment, hunger and homelessness to name a few. I know these are BIG problems, but I can't help but believe that with all the technology being developed, we can't connect people who are hungry and out of work with training to fill available, entry-level tech jobs.

This idea has the potential to take a large segment of low-opportunity youth, women and adults and transform their lives from one of meager existence to one in which they can earn a living wage, successfully care for their families and create wealth in the communities in which they live.

Can you imagine a new paradigm in which all able-bodied Americans could be trained to work in tech? Imagine the new ideas and ways to solve problems that could not come from any other source than from those who had to live it, be creative, or die? I can see it!

Of course, it would take a huge, collective effort and lots of resources to bring this idea to fruition. But we have a lot of what we need already developed and available; the concept just needs the dollars to grow it to scale. The funds are available; they just need to be pooled and managed for optimum effectiveness.

Since a lack of diversity doesn't exist in the tech sector alone, other industries need to weigh in, take a seat at the table, open up their checkbooks, and help to solve this problem.

SOME ARE FIGHTING THE GOOD FIGHT

There are definitely some corporate leaders in this fight who are playing an active role in concert with NCWIT and other organizations. They are strategic and investment partners who validate the work NCWIT is doing to diversify the IT talent pipeline.

Their level of investment is significantly helping to broaden the conversation. We just need more of them to bring about true change. These companies' logos grace the NCWIT website and all reports and other collateral pieces disseminated across the country.

Why? Not because they want to toot their own horns. Rather, they offer their brands so that others can see how committed they are and will want to join them in the effort to improve life in America for millions of people.

Because of their strong support, these are the firms who will be recognized as the change leaders. They are strengthening their brands as favorable companies in which to work and with which to associate. Their employees are becoming individual change agents, utilizing their time and talents to serve the greater good. In turn, I hope they become the companies of choice in their industries from whom we buy products and services necessary in business and in life. Apple, Google, AT&T, Bank of America, Microsoft, Merck, Intel, Bloomberg, and Hewlett-Packard are among those organizations.

POSITIVE BRANDING
While enhancing their brand is not the impetus for the work they do or the dollars they contribute,

improving public perception does become a natural by-product.

When I am in need of products or services for my business or home, I intentionally seek out those who are working and adding value in the areas I care deeply about. Increasing the number of women and people of color in technology is an issue I care deeply about. Why? Because it has the potential to change lives, put people to work, and solve a whole host of other societal problems.

A new initiative launched by the Women's Business Enterprise National Council (WBENC), the certification gold standard for women-owned businesses is "Act Intentional." Quite simply, we intentionally purchase goods and services from corporations who buy from women-owned businesses. Imagine the tremendous impact on the market if the millions of women-owned businesses did that.

If companies care about their brand awareness, taking part in efforts to solve so many problems, as well as perpetuating a sense of fairness, will greatly enhance that brand. In fact, the Public Affairs budgets of major corporations include a very healthy philanthropy component. These are the funds earmarked for non-profit organizations that further causes such as the arts, education, culture and civic/ social justice.

However, the healthier portion of corporations' budgets earmarked to enhance brand awareness and market penetration is not tied to social causes, but rather to marketing. While both combine to form a company's "identity," this is one issue that also needs to tap the larger share of corporations' spendable dollars—advertising and marketing.

Imagine being known as the company that utilized its available resources to tackle unemployment, homelessness, hunger, and helping millions of Americans live a better life? I don't know about you, but that is certainly the company I'd want to associate with or for whom to work. That's also the company with whom I would spend my dollars for goods or services they might sell. I would also invest in their stock.

Isn't that the reaction for which any company would invest dearly? Especially one that is publicly traded? I think so.

So how do we get corporations on board? How do we get them to care enough to stop admiring the problem and actually DO something about it?

At NCWIT, we've been working hard for 12 years to get companies, foundations and wealthy individuals invested and involved. Thankfully, some have responded. However, we need *all* companies to step up to achieve a bigger and broader impact. Otherwise, it could take another 20 years to attain the level of change so desperately needed. We do not have two decades to get this done.

GETTING THE MEDIA INVOLVED

It's evident that a mainstream media push is war-ranted—in which everyone, everywhere could receive the same message. It would contain the following talking points:

- We have a significant wealth gap in America
- Too many Americans are unemployed or under-employed
- Corporations are creating 1.2 million new tech jobs over the next few years
- These are high-paying jobs
- We can train people to do some of these jobs
- We need to educate more girls and people of color in preparation for these jobs
- We are doing something about this problem
- We are (insert your company name here) Corporation; working for a better future...

How about that for brand awareness?

DIVERSITY BOOSTS THE BOTTOM LINE

What if working for a better future or brand awareness isn't your thing? How about stronger profits? Would that float your boat? I'm guessing, yes. Yes, it would.

Did you know that studies have shown that companies with more diverse boards, inclusive of women, have a greater record of profitability than those without women on their board?

Customers do a lot more due diligence these days when it comes to making purchases. Of course, we know that women make an overwhelming percentage of purchase decisions. So, it is not surprising to learn that when looking to make a purchase, consumers are more likely to do so from a company who has a more inclusive culture and commitment to diversity.

As I've mentioned before, I was blessed to spend my eleven corporate years in a very inclusive and welcoming environment. At Exxon, I had ample mentors and examples of diverse leadership and management. I always felt welcomed and valued. My managers always treated me with respect and seemed genuinely pleased to have me around.

What's more, they nurtured my entrepreneurial spirit and allowed me to be creative, resourceful and action-oriented. When I decided to branch out on my own, they were very supportive and became one of my first corporate customers.

Did this type of inclusive culture factor into their becoming the largest corporation in the world? (Exxon was the #1 company on the Fortune 500 list during my entire period of employment and well after.) I'd like to think so. Sure, they sold an awful lot of petroleum and related products, but valuing your most important asset—your workforce—is vitally important to financial success as well.

You can produce the best product in the world, but if you don't have a committed, loyal and satisfied workforce to sell and service your products, your financial results will suffer. From my recollection, the associates I knew from Exxon all seemed very satisfied in their relationship with their employer.

In fact, it was not uncommon for me to frequently meet people who had been employed by Exxon for over 30 years. Who knows? If I hadn't decided to become an entrepreneur 32 years ago, I might still be at Exxon myself. Might even be the CEO!

Positive financial results are a critical element in the success of every company. It is senior management's responsibility to deliver excellent shareholder value. Their compensation is based on achieving good results. If they consistently fall short of their objectives, they are typically fired, forced to retire, or replaced.

If companies can improve their financial results by fostering a more inclusive and diverse workplace, why wouldn't they want to invest the necessary resources to ensure that objective is achieved? They should. This should be a critical leadership imperative upon which compensation should also be based.

Corporate diversity goals and objectives should be established and metrics developed to measure how effective senior leaders are in achieving these goals. When goals are tied to compensation, they stand a better than average chance of being realized.

Imagine if *EVERY* U.S. corporation was focused on increasing the participation of women and people of color in its workforce? We would cease to have a problem, and I could go on to the next issue that needs my attention!

CHAPTER 7

THE DEFINITION OF INSANITY

*Doing the same things the same way you've
always done them and expecting different results.*

Business as usual used to be a somewhat positive state of being, but not so anymore. Businesses can neither afford to stagnate nor cease to innovate. By the same token, attracting and retaining good talent should be one of the most critical imperatives of every corporation.

Since we already know that too few women enter the technical workforce, and those who do subsequently leave it 56 percent of the time, it's critical that we change the game and do something drastically different if businesses are to survive.

Let me be clear. *Doing nothing is not an option; it's the definition of insanity.*

Sadly, that's exactly what many companies are doing—*nothing*—and that doesn't bode well for our collective future.

Too often, I speak with IT executives who boast about a local school or program they support as if that by itself will solve this problem. I promptly applaud their efforts and encourage them to continue that support. However, I also let them know the importance of them becoming active on a national level. Without that level of effort, it will take forever to move the national needle and effect any meaningful change.

Many get that, but moving a large corporation to take action can take years. We don't have years...

Surprisingly, others prefer to bury their heads in the sand or engage in the game of *Kick the Can*, thinking they'll let the next guy do it. They are either too busy or too disengaged to care.

So what does "business as usual" look like? Or what can be the potential outcomes of doing nothing?

Well, first there's the real probability of a continued and steady decline of women in the technical workforce. We know that there was a high of 37 percent of technical women in the workforce in the mid-1980s. That number is 26 percent today—a significant decline over the last 30 years.

What happened???

We weren't paying attention, and therefore did nothing to stem the slide. Logic dictates that if we continue to do nothing, the decline will worsen over time. And, as we've already covered, that's not good for a whole host of reasons.

Principally, the absence of women and people of color in the design and invention of technology will continue to lead us down the path of invention devoid of the richness and fabric that diverse populations offer.

Imagine the ability to capture the creativity and richness of diverse cultures into technological design? How much better could it be? Or, how about solving problems from a woman's perspective? It would be different, no question. I, for one, long for that deeper, richer technology.

My belief is that so do all companies competing in this global economy. Therefore, it's everyone's responsibility to do what is necessary to stem the decline of technical women in the workforce. We can't pass the buck or think someone else is going to do something. This is going to take a huge effort to ensure the effective development of a diverse pipeline so we can see a reverse of the decline.

* * * * *

There aren't enough women in senior IT positions. There, I said it!

I have the honor of meeting corporate CIOs all across this country. To date, only five of them have been female; only one has been an African-American female. That's pretty depressing.

When I inquire how many of a CIOs direct reports are women or people of color, the response is a bit better, but certainly nothing to write home about.

So, another outcome of doing nothing means a continued dearth of women and people of color serving in senior IT leadership positions. This creates a circular problem—women like to see other women in positions to which they can aspire. If women can't see themselves rising in a corporation, they will leave. They also can't attract more women to work there, and around and around it goes.

Thus, just as important as it is to attract women into the workforce, it is also critical to develop that talent by offering "stretch" assignments, sponsoring and advocating on their behalf, and providing a culture that allows them to thrive. Stretch assignments are those that may be just outside a person's current skill set or capabilities.

When I worked for Exxon, I was promoted regularly. It was a wonderful culture that afforded me the ability to move around the company and gain experiences that shaped and developed me into the person I have become.

Does that culture still exist today in U.S. corporations? I have visited some where it is quite evident that it does. People are happy, loyal and dedicated to excellence in their work. They care about each other and don't have any qualms about showing it.

* * * * *

During a recent business trip, an associate and I were struck by the sheer happiness on display at a local IHOP. Now granted, this was by no means a technical environment, which made it even more mind-blowing.

We were seated at one of the booths that looked right behind the counter where the food was cooked and all the workers congregated. First of all, there had to be ten people back there (quite a lot, I thought).

Secondly, the crew was very diverse, speaking multiple languages and representing a variety of cultures.

Third, they seemed more like a family than a workgroup. I started paying attention when a female crew member arrived for work and joined the others. She was genuinely happy to be there, giving and receiving hugs from the other members of the crew.

People stopped flipping pancakes or making coffee to greet her.

Our server, an older Hispanic gentleman, was just delightful, taking very good care of us and ensuring we got the best pancake and egg deal available.

This was an extremely happy workplace. I had never seen anything like it in a traditionally low-wage environment. In fact, it is usually just the opposite—people unhappy about their station in life and bringing that attitude to work.

On the flip side, these people actually loved each other and were happy to be at work. It showed in how they treated the customers and how they carried out their responsibilities.

Needless to say, the food was wonderful and the place was packed!

A happy, collaborative workplace isn't the case everywhere, however. In fact, in many environments, just the opposite is true. Empty cubicles stand as a monument to frequent reorganizations and reductions in force, with no replacements budgeted in the foreseeable future. Morale is low, and everybody is overworked and tense. This shows in their lack of support for each other.

We need more women and people of color to break through to senior leadership positions throughout the corporation, but especially in IT. It would have a definite impact on the culture of an organization. We have witnessed, and it is very well documented, that when women lead, positive results happen.

I wonder if the manager of that IHOP in Orlando is a woman? What makes that such a happy workplace?

RELYING ON OFFSHORE TALENT

Some companies have attempted to solve their workforce issues by developing an over-reliance on offshore talent. I'm here to tell you, that doesn't work either. In fact, it only compounds the problem. It provides a false sense of accomplishment that the jobs are being filled and the work is getting done. However, we are still dealing with a homogenous group of people who have been taught to think and act the same way. As a result, the technology they design and develop won't have the added value of diverse thought and perspective.

What's more, sending jobs overseas won't help to alleviate the problems of unemployment, hunger, homelessness and crime that are at epic proportions in some parts of this country. As I've said before, being trained to work in IT and having access to a good salary will go a long way in stamping out some of our social ills in this country.

I know there's an economic benefit to companies to offshore IT jobs to Asia and Europe, where the wages are lower, but at what cost to the U.S.? If companies could allot a percentage of those jobs for American citizens, provide training and a positive environment within which to work, the country as a whole would be so much better off.

Below are some interesting outsourcing statistics:

Total number of U.S. jobs offshore outsourced in 2013	2,637,239
Percent of CFOs surveyed who said their firm was currently offshoring outsourcing	36 %
Percent of CFOs who favored India for outsourcing	26 %
Percent of CFOs who favored China for outsourcing	18 %
Offshore Outsourcing By Sector	**Percent of Companies**
Manufacturing	53 %
IT Services	43 %
R&D	38 %
Distribution	26 %
Call or Help Centers	12 %
Reasons Why Companies Outsource (Multiple Answers Allowed)	**Percent**
Reduce or control costs	44 %
Gain access to IT resources unavailable internally	34 %
Free up internal resources	31 %
Improve business or customer focus	28 %
Accelerate company reorganization / transformation	22 %
Accelerate project	15 %
Gain access to management expertise unavailable internally	15 %
Reduce time to market	9 %

BRING THE JOBS BACK, TRAIN URBAN YOUTH

If we could bring one-tenth of those jobs back to the U.S. in areas with high unemployment, it would go a long way toward ending the downward spiral of hopelessness in some communities and set people on a path of life-changing proportions.

Urban centers are ripe with citizens who can be trained to code, perform quality assurance, customer service, and other entry-level IT tasks. I've seen many programs work successfully over the years in cities like New York and Newark, NJ.

For example, Technology High School in Newark, NJ, offers a course from Verizon that teaches urban youth how to become network technicians. Another course from Cisco teaches interested students how to become Cisco-certified network engineers.

These skills (which usually cost dearly to acquire in the open market), have the potential to set these kids up with skills for life, putting them on a path to earn a good living and gain access to employment at some of the country's largest corporations.

Absent such early opportunities, these same youths, faced with limited choices and excluded from achieving the American dream, can spend a lifetime performing menial jobs, or worse, end up on the wrong side of the law. It costs far more to support inmates in the penal system than it does to train an individual to earn a living wage.

What's more, we need to access this vital source of untapped talent hidden in communities all across the nation to fill jobs that are going unfilled. Every time I have the honor of speaking to students—be they high school or college level—I am amazed at the level of promise these young people possess. They only lack access to opportunities, just like many diverse business owners I have met over the last 30 years.

There's a real disconnect here. Companies continue to create hundreds of thousands of tech jobs right here in America that run the risk of going unfilled due to the lack of talent. At the same time, untapped talent exists in many urban communities of color all across the nation. Why can't we bridge that gap and solve these two critical problems at the same time?

How, you ask. In my entrepreneurial mind, it's quite simple, actually. And, it can be done with a targeted, focused and diligent effort. Here's how I see it:

1. Identify the national platform/infrastructure that can manage the program via a hub-and-spoke structure. To be sure, we won't solve the problem utilizing hundreds of small, locally based programs that don't interact or communicate with each other, typically re-inventing the wheel and not leveraging available resources. They are usually so busy fundraising to stay afloat, that their impact often gets marginalized.

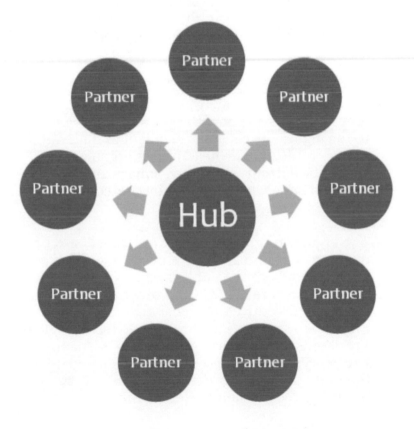

- This should not be a government agency, rather a public-private partnership that can enlist the aid and support of both government and the private sector. It has to be small enough to be nimble, creative and entrepreneurial; able to take necessary action without being burdened by layers of bureaucracy.

However, it must be large enough to have the scale to succeed in its mission. Talent is key! It is imperative we get the right folks with the right skillsets driving change in this organization.

This entity must be equipped to get the job done. That means selecting the right leadership from the private sector, having sufficient funding so that fundraising is not job one, and gaining access to the highest levels of government and private industry. Ideally, the head of this organization should be entrepreneurial, visionary and passionate—someone who has a demonstrated track record of success.

The organization should have a strong board of directors/advisors that have incredible reach and influence in both the public and private sectors. I envision corporate CEOs and other high-ranking corporate executives sitting side by side with municipal, state and federal executives, as well as Presidents of colleges and universities. All are necessary to chart the course, effect change in their environments, and leverage their influence to further the mission of the organization.

I'd almost like to see this structured as a for-profit entity; recognizing that a profit margin drives a strong adherence to setting and achieving objectives. In order for this to happen, though, it will need to be funded via the private sector and not reliant upon government grants I'm not against establishing a non-profit structure, however, if that is the easiest path to funding.

2. Secondly, the mission should be simple and straightforward—identify the skills and talents corporations need to fill their jobs, and establish the training programs and methods of identifying potential candidates who can be trained to be successful in those jobs.

   The open tech jobs you see on every major job board or on company websites are typically not unique to any one company. In essence, companies need people who can learn to code in a variety of programming languages, provide technical support for hardware or software, perform quality assurance processes, analyze business needs, interface with customers, etc.

   We need to solicit all required skills needed by corporations all across the country in order to develop or leverage existing curricula to train/ hone those skills in the target population. Soft skills training will also be required as it is naive to think that people who have never worked in a corporate environment before will automatically know how to successfully assimilate into one without proper guidance and coaching.

3. Next, we need to identify the partners who
    provide this type of training today in order to
    create the spoke component of the solution.
    Potential partners could include universities,
    community colleges, for-profit training organiza-
    tions, non-profit entities, and so on.

    I would venture to say that there are thousands of
    such organizations across the country that could
    be involved in this national initiative, eliminating
    the need and expense of creating them. We would
    only need to create and launch such a program in
    communities where they do not presently exist.

    Once the partners are identified, they will be
    'franchised' to operate within this new structure
    of program delivery. It will be important to
    establish consistent guidelines across the country
    to ensure we can achieve a uniform delivery of
    instruction and coaching.

    If there are unique parameters that a company
    needs to incorporate, they can pay more for that
    required degree of customization. If not, the
    program would guarantee a pre-set list of deliver-
    ables agreed upon in advance.

    By working directly with corporations, this new
    entity will clearly understand what is needed to
    succeed in each environment in order to identify
    the best candidates. This will, in essence, become
    the feeder into a corporation's IT pipeline and
    used to support the need for entry-level talent.

    An important element that needs to be incorpo-
    rated to ensure a greater degree of success is
    ongoing coaching throughout a new employee's
    initial year of employment at a client firm.

Learning a new technical skill is only part of the equation. A new employee must also know how to navigate and assimilate into a new environment. The coaching will aid new employees to do just that, while at the same time, help them avoid the pitfalls and political undercurrents inherent in all corporate cultures.

4. The pricing structure would need to be established to support the needs of the organization. I envision corporations paying an annual fee for training and recruitment. The fee could vary based on any number of parameters, such as size, number of employees, number of geographic locations, number of open requirements, degree of customization, and so on.

The more corporations participating, the more the costs can be shared. What I haven't figured out is how to encourage *ALL* U.S. corporations to participate. From my many years working with NCWIT, I've seen firsthand how few companies actually do anything to solve this issue. Somehow, this has got to be mandated. Maybe this is where the government comes in. Perhaps a new regulation stipulating that all companies doing business with either Federal, State or Local government agencies must become part of this initiative.

On the other hand, regulation only goes so far. Perhaps some sort of merit system would work well here. Certainly, the business case can be made as to how corporations would positively impact their bottom lines by participating in this initiative. The cost of recruiting and training skilled talent is high when done internally.

Outsourcing these tasks to a lower-cost solution provider will help to lower the overall cost of talent acquisition.

By participating in this broad, national initiative, companies can be viewed as caring about solving the problem. They can extend their brand as a company who values diversity in the tech pipeline. They can also stop dealing a few dollars here and there trying to effect change. Finally, they will be able to make a meaningful investment to derive positive results.

Yes, broad adoption will be key to closing the skills gap in this country. There are some very large corporations doing incredible things, but they are few and far between. Others are only driving a very small amount of local change, and that won't cut it. We need everyone to participate on a national level—and we need them now.

5. To make this concept widely known, it will be key to have national, mainstream media attention. This problem is bigger than the tech industry and needs to become a widely known national imperative, much like poverty, hunger or homelessness.

* * * * *

This discussion reminds me of the many times a corporation has asked me if they would get "diversity credit" for doing business with us. My official response was, "I don't know what that means," hoping they would get the message that getting quality technical services at a greater value should be all the "credit" they should want and need.

Unfortunately, companies need to have a financial incentive to do the right thing. I understand the need to be profit-driven. I really do. I've been profit-driven for more than three decades. Unfortunately, companies still have difficulty in making the connection between doing *well* and doing *good*. However, if we are going to close the wealth and opportunity gaps that exist in this country, the entire tech industry will need to play a role. That means creating and implementing this solution must take priority over profit and competitive positioning for a while.

As someone who has been blessed with vision, I spend a good deal of time imagining how things can be—in life, in business and in the world. In my mind's eye, I see the industry coming together in a mighty collaborative, investing the necessary funds and resources to identify, train, employ and retain all current and prospective tech workers.

I see thriving communities where today only urban blight exists. I see children of every race and color learning computer science principles from elementary school on up through high school graduation. I see financial aid being made available for students desirous of going to college but are economically disadvantaged and unable to afford it on their own.

But, most importantly, I see advances in technology and innovation that will astound us. Who knows what the imagination and creativity of those new to the game will develop. When you think differently, you approach problems differently. Designing solutions differently will drive innovation like we've not seen before. We can ill afford to not tap into this under-utilized brainpower; we've got way too much to lose.

I promise you, there is hidden genius in communities all across America. I have seen it, judged it, and been completely blown away by it.

For example, the #YesWeCode Hackathon that took place during the 25th Annual Essence Festival in New Orleans was amazing. Teams came from all across the country and were predominantly African-American teenagers. They were asked to create a solution to a social problem.

The distinguished panel of judges, of which I was honored to be a member, had difficulty deciding between the apps to stop human trafficking, stop bullying, or a better way for diabetics to get their glucose readings. In a word, we were simply amazed!

These young people scrimped and scraped just to make it to "The Big Easy" from all over the country.

Many had never coded before, or had ever left their hometown. They didn't know each other, but were grouped into teams.

This was innovation in motion, and everyone was passionately committed to finding the hidden genius we know exists in our communities.

Whatever it costs to fix this problem, we need to spend it. It will be worth every penny!

CHAPTER 8

SUPERHEROES TO THE RESCUE!

Be the change you want to see in the world.

To be sure, there is a lot of work to be done. There are people living in poverty in urban pockets all across our nation. There are thousands of single mothers who can't afford to work because their lack of skill only lets them take low-paying jobs that won't cover their basic needs like transportation, childcare and food.

Men who haven't stayed in school and acquired marketable skills are also at risk. Unemployment numbers in urban areas are typically 3 to 4 times the national average.

Americans living in rural areas and on tribal lands have also been shut out of the tech boom. Hopelessness is an awful thing to live with; it robs people of their joy and instills in them a hard heart.

One of my favorite coffeetable books is *I Dream A World* by Brian Lanker. It is a compilation of photographs and interviews of Black women who changed America. It depicts heroes of times past who decided not to be victims of their circumstances, but rather blaze trails for themselves and others to follow.

In the book's foreword, poet Maya Angelou salutes these women—some famous, others you may never have heard of—as an outstanding representation of the human race. She writes:

> *"Black women are blessed with heart breaking tenderness and majestic strength that speak of the heroic survival of a people who were stolen into subrogation, denied chastity and refused innocence."*

How true!

NO ONE LEFT BEHIND

That book inspired me—and I, too, dream a world. In my world—once and for all—no one is being left behind. Not women, not people of color, not the disabled nor returning military, and certainly not children.

I dream a world in which in every school across the nation, children are being taught age-appropriate computing skills from kindergarten through college. They are being taught to reason and to develop logical thinking, which can be brought to bear to solve problems. In each grade, they build upon the skills learned in the previous year. The problems become more complex every semester. These young people are taught to design algorithms and code, using existing models, and/or creating new ones.

They are working in teams with their classmates, reasoning with each other, listening to and respecting one another's opinions and input. They are eager to hear what everyone has to say. Differences of opinion are welcomed because these encourage teams to explore the solution from varied perspectives.

Girls are just as engaged as the boys. They always provide a different way of looking at and solving problems. Culture and ethnicity play a big role in how problems are approached. The diverse teams are eager to know how each culture represented in the group would solve the problem.

In the early tech days, it was common for ideas and companies to be formed in college (or in garages). Many of the companies worth billions today started in humble surroundings. Here are a few:

- Facebook was created by Mark Zuckerberg and others while still students at Harvard.
- Apple was created by Steve Jobs and Steve Wozniak in the Jobs' family garage.
- Larry Page and Sergey Brin paid $1,700 a month to rent Carol Wojcicki's garage while they were

students at Stanford. That garage was the birthplace of Google.

- Michael Dell started his PC business, Dell, in his dorm room during his freshman year at the University of Texas, Austin.

- The idea for Twitter was born at a San Francisco park.

You get the idea ...

In my world, innovative ideas could be formed as early as high school. College years could be used to refine the ideas, utilize them as class projects, develop the business case and seek funding to bring them to market.

The flow of new design and innovative technology would be tremendous. Everything from improving existing methods of doing things to building a better mousetrap. It would be a time where the worlds of business and education both collaborated and collided, with very positive outcomes.

We know some of our very mature systems in this country are broken—Social Security, the "too big to fail" financial market, education, healthcare, and Homeland Security, to name a few. I don't see a pathway to fixing them anytime soon, do you? In this present age, we don't have enough political will to do so.

What we will need (other than the political resolve) is the mindshare of problem solvers who have been trained and encouraged to think from a very young age. We'll need collaborators people who know how to work in teams and appreciate the diversity of thought that cross-gendered and culturally rich groups bring to the table.

What we won't need are lifelong politicians getting in the way of innovation by refusing to be part of the solution if it doesn't come from their side of the aisle. What we can't afford is the withholding of funding to study and fix these problems while people stamp their feet and loudly proclaim that they can probably come up with a better idea with a little more time and money, so they can't support the one on the table.

We see where that has gotten us. To be clear, it certainly won't move us forward to real fixes in this lifetime.

WHAT DO WE DO IN THE MEANTIME?

Well, it's going to take a couple of generations to achieve that level of talent. So, what do we do in the meantime? Give up? Maintain the status quo? Continue increasing the opportunity and wealth gap in this country? I say NO!!

In my world, I see us utilizing the "buy it while we build it" methodology. There are many reasons for utilizing this mindset; it costs less and gets you to the market faster.

This scenario is used every day by businesses all over the world. For instance, when a tech giant wants to fill a gap in its technology roadmap, what do they do? It acquires a company that has created the product it needs for millions and sometimes billions of dollars.

There are many examples of this phenomenon over just the last few years. Here's a few you may remember:

- Facebook acquired WhatsApp for $19 billion (2014) and Instagram for $1 billion (2012).
- Google acquired Motorola Mobility for $12.5 billion (2012) and YouTube for $1.65 billion (2006).
- Apple acquired Dr. Dre's Beats Headphones for $3.2 billion (2014).
- Microsoft acquired Skype for $8.5 billion (2011) and Nokia for $7.2 billion (2013).
- Yahoo acquired Tumblr for $1.1 billion (2013).
- Ebay acquired PayPal for $1.5 billion (2002).

Yep! That's how the big boys do it in Silicon Valley.

They could have invested the money to develop similar technology, but realized it would be far less time-consuming and far less expensive to just buy what they needed. So, they did. This happens all the time.

Imagine if that same methodology was used to acquire the talent needed to fill (too many to count) open tech jobs? What if the six companies above (or their very wealthy founders) each invested just $100 million and were joined by some of their peers who aren't listed above, but have very healthy acquisition track records of their own, to do the same.

With that kind of funding—potentially $1 billion —into the national infrastructure that currently exists, we could solve the "scarce tech talent" problem within the next couple of years.

In my mind, if you can invest a billion dollars to buy new technology, but won't make a much smaller investment to develop the languishing talent pool who haven't been given the opportunity to succeed in the marketplace, something is very wrong.

The best technology in the world can't run by itself. It needs the talent to make it go, to make it better, faster, cooler—to come up with the next big thing.

Imagine what that amount of funding could do!

Well, for one, everyone who can be trained for a career in tech would be. The marketplace can absorb thousands of newly trained recruits across the entire tech spectrum—from tech support to software engineering—and everything in between.

Some would need more training than others. That is to be expected with the wide range of available talent being under-utilized today. Some will need soft skills and other remedial types of training, but that doesn't mean there wouldn't be a job they could perform.

Some of this knowledge can be attained remotely via online classes, but for many, training will have to be done in a structured format at an accessible location with classroom facilities, all across the country.

Childcare and stipends to cover transportation and daily living expenses would need to be made available to all trainees. After all, people still have to eat, live and take care of their children while they are learning a new skill.

With $1 billion of funding, that would not be a problem.

* * * * *

The mere fact that there are still over 4.4 billion people in the world without Internet access is very troublesome to me. Until that situation is remedied, they will continue to be victims of the "Digital Divide." What is needed to bridge that gap for many in developing countries is money, infrastructure and incentive.

In the U.S., some 50 million people still don't access the Internet. In some parts of the country, the same challenges exist as in developing countries where people are off the grid (about 7 percent). According to a Pew Research report, the vast majority of Americans who don't access the Internet cite that it is because it is too hard or they feel it isn't relevant to them.

Think of what they are missing, and what hidden genius *we* may be missing from their absence. We have to find a way to connect with them as well. Ninety-three percent of 50 million is a lot of people!

In addition to training, childcare, transportation and stipends, newly trained recruits will need a job. And, it can't take six months or more for one to be made available to them.

Companies with job openings and specific job requirements must be identified so that recruits can receive those specific skills during their training. Knowing there is a good-paying job waiting for them if they complete their training is a huge incentive to persevere when the going gets tough.

The good news is that we've done a ton of research in this space and have learned a lot about this issue.

There are hundreds, if not thousands, of local programs across the country focused on STEM (Science-Technology-Engineering-Math). However, if these programs are *not* connected to a national infrastructure like NCWIT, their efforts will unfortunately continue to have minimum impact.

That said, with $1 billion dollars in funding, all those institutions could be connected and enabled to reach the masses and fill up their local classrooms.

If we're going to reach parity and solve this problem in the next ten years, we have got to start making quantum leaps now. We need to establish that funding model now and not waste another minute.

There are so many women and people of color who could benefit from learning computing skills and earning a living wage in good, high-paying jobs.

It would make a huge difference ... in my world.

Wipe out unemployment? *Check!*

Homelessness? *Check!*

Hunger? *Check!*

Hopelessness? *Check!*

Fill all the job openings? *Check!*

Solve the problems associated with Social Security, healthcare, education, financial markets, Homeland Security? *Check!*

I like the view from my world. It's not a dream... and has a very real opportunity to become reality.

We know what needs to be done and have been working on it for over ten years.

We can fix this WHEN we work together.

CHAPTER 9

A BRIGHTER FUTURE

Own your tomorrows.

B efore we start sitting in support of technical women, it's important to not lose sight of the fact that we need more seats at all tables—the design table, the board table, and the decision-making table.

It's not enough to just add women and people of color to the tech workforce. It's imperative to actively ensure they assume positions of leadership and engage in ever increasing decision making.

Unfortunately, too few directors of corporate boards are women or people of color. Consequently, decisions being made at those board tables are missing the perspectives, desires and needs of diverse constituents—employees, customers, suppliers and the broader community at large.

When that happens, decisions are made in a vacuum without regard for the potential impact that could adversely affect the diverse community. We see the results of that lack of sensitivity in the current disparity that exists in the workforce, in leadership positions and in the number of diverse suppliers engaged in the procurement of goods and services in this country.

This concept seems to be clearly understood when it comes to attracting younger generations to the workforce and as consumers. We recognize that new ideas are necessary to engage members of Gen Y and Millennials who don't work or interact the same way as Baby Boomers.

New-age advertising ideas to attract young consumers have been in play for years now and are constantly being refreshed as new insights are gained on this critical demographic. Similarly, to attract more women and people of color to the tech work-force, New-Age ideas are equally as critical. We won't be successful doing things the way we've always done them.

Years ago, the common cry from major U.S. corporations was they couldn't find qualified minority-owned companies with whom to do busi-ness. It became their fallback position when asked why their procurement with diverse firms was so low. (As a leading advocate of supplier diversity, I was often one of those asking the question.) I heard that response so much, it made my head (and my heart) hurt.

You see, I knew there were qualified diverse firms in pretty much every commodity category a company would need. I also knew that when I heard that response, the company was not sincere in turning around its dismal performance. So the pat response, "We can't find..." became a much-used crutch.

I hear a lot of the same response today when asking companies about their lack of women and people of color in their tech workforce:

- "We can't find women and people of color to hire..."
- "We go to the best schools to recruit and there are very few women or minorities to choose from..."
- "There's a pipeline issue that's bigger than us..."
- "We don't have any senior women leaders now to promote to CIO, CTO or other tech leadership positions..."

Such refrains are also heard when companies are called to task about the lack of women and people of color on their board. Maybe it's because I know so many talented, committed, and experienced diverse business owners, but I would think that major corporate boards would be clamoring for the real-world experiences, problem-solving abilities, persistence and perseverance a seasoned, diverse business owner could bring to the table.

So often, these skills are more entrenched, born out of adversity, from busting through roadblocks or pushing through resistance to survive, than those inherent in lifelong corporate executives.

I would think corporations would be banging our doors down to gain market insight and other critical success factors from our perspective. However, that's just not the case. Instead, the same few diverse corporate directors are recycled and reused over and over again, bringing the same corporate perspective already at the board table.

It really makes you wonder. Do they really want to attract fresh ideas and new perspectives, or do they really want to maintain the status quo, which admittedly, is a lot easier to do?

It absolutely requires great executive leadership to move a corporation in a different direction. Since policy is set at the board table, it's imperative that change agents and diversity advocates take their rightful place at the table.

We've earned the right. Now it's time to "have a seat!"

That seat comes with a lot of responsibility, however. We can't just sit quietly and not provide the valuable experience and expertise we are known for or that got us there. Ours may be the only voice that moves the corporation down a different path—one that's more inclusive and innovative as a result. It is our responsibility to speak, act, and move at the appropriate times.

Once we get our seat, we must do something with it, or we are just taking up space. And, there's a lot of that going on already!

Some things that need to be implemented at the board level to inspire change are:

1. Assess where the corporation is investing its financial assets. You can tell what's important to a company by understanding where it puts its money.

2. Assess the executive leadership make-up along with 2 to 3 levels down from the C-suite—would a photo of this group look like the world in which we live today or the signers of the Declaration of Independence?

3. Request a review of college and professional recruiting strategies—the target schools for campus recruiting—are they just Ivy League/Top Ten or is there a healthy number of HBCUs and MSIs in the mix? Do these strategies include community and technical schools?

4. Request a talent map. Where do women and minorities factor in? Is there at least 30 percent in the top five levels of the corporation? Are there development plans in place to advance more into the upper ranks?

These are just four things I would request as a board member to establish a baseline. Once these are established and fully known, then objectives can be set in every area of the company. Unless it starts at this level, real change will always be just beyond reach.

CHAPTER 10

THIS IS WHAT SUCCESS LOOKS LIKE

True success becomes reality when a passion for success overpowers the fear of failure.

Success. The word has multiple definitions in the dictionary.

The accomplishment of an aim or purpose...

The attainment of popularity or profit...

The fact of getting or achieving wealth, respect, or fame...

If you were to ask me what success means, I would have to shamelessly borrow this line from Maya Angelou:

"Success is liking yourself, liking what you do, and liking how you do it."

It has been three decades since I embarked on this adventure, a journey that has taken me to amazing highs and gut-wrenching lows. Throughout this journey, I would have to say that my experiences have been about being true to myself and the people around me, loving every moment of the journey and feeling that I gave my best along every step of the way.

For those of you who have waited until this part of the book to hear my magic recipe or how-tos for success, I would have to say that there is no simple formula for success. However, I can share with you a few attributes that helped me break the mold and go off into uncharted territories.

IT ALL STARTS WITH FEARLESSNESS!

For an African-American woman who grew up with very little, I had already achieved "success" beyond my wildest dreams. I was working for a Fortune 50 company, I was making good money, I was getting promoted and I was selling early technology on Wall Street. I had already broken a few barriers. But I did not want to settle. I wanted more. I did not know what more meant or what it looked like, but I was determined to find out.

The thread of fearlessness cannot stop after you launch your business. You've got to own it and be proud of it at every stage. In my more than thirty years of being an entrepreneur, I have seen economic highs and lows. Businesses being enthusiastic about buying technology and also freezing all spending. And once you are an entrepreneur, you have your team to take care of, so you can never show fear.

I still have this fearless streak in me. In fact, I just expanded my business to the Far East and set up an office in Singapore. Do I know much about the Far East? Not yet. Do I have a lot of connections there? No! But I know business is booming around the Pacific Rim and I want to be part of that growth.

DON'T OVERANALYZE YOUR DECISIONS

We are all born with a gut instinct. That little voice in our head that tells us whether we are right or wrong; whether we should do something or not. Listen to it.

Throughout my years in business, I have trusted my instincts. You need to do that. I would not be expanding my business to Singapore if I did not trust my gut. Doubting yourself or overanalyzing leads to a loss of opportunities. If you don't grab what is in front of you, someone else will. Don't let that happen.

KEEP THE IDEAS FLOWING

Starting your business is sometimes the easy part. Actually, it is the easy part! Keeping the business relevant over a thirty-year time frame is challenging. You have to keep thinking up new ideas all the time. Listen to your customers. Study your competition. Make feedback your best friend. Hearing bad feedback may hurt, but it will make you think through issues and generate more ideas.

My customer base has changed over the years. And when I see today's generation of customers wanting to do business with me, just like their counterparts from many years ago, I know I am relevant. I know I have transformed, and I know my ideas are evolving and finding acceptance.

STAY IN THE GAME!

Stay in the game! *Stay in the game!* Do you hear me? I can't say it any louder! You want to know what has happened to me? In the 32 years I've been a business woman, I've seen personal and professional devastation. Life events that would make you just want to quit and walk away. Don't do it.

I lost 30 percent of my customers after 9/11. Did I quit? *NO!*

One of my customers filed the largest bankruptcy in US history. Did I quit? *NO!*

I had a heart attack in 2007. Did I quit? *NO!*

Not only did I *not* quit, I emerged stronger. You will want to quit many, many times. You will want to go into hibernation. Don't do it; hang in there instead.

DON'T UNDERESTIMATE THE ROLE OF A MENTOR

From my early days in Corporate America, mentorship has been an integral part of my life. My early career mentor was instrumental in recognizing that I could sell and launched me on a new career trajectory. I've had several corporate "champions" over the years who have made significant contributions to my success. Today, I surround myself with coaches who support multiple facets of my life.

Think about the people who have made a difference in your life. Who pushed you into unfamiliar terrain? Who was your loudest cheerleader? Who stood in the background silently backing you? Find those people. Embrace them in your life. And accept coaching every step along the way.

When you are successful, people will ask you to mentor them. Give back generously and create successes to come after you.

SUCCESS IS NOT ALL ABOUT THE MONEY

Business success stories, especially in the technology sector, are studded with "financial riches" stories. Every time you turn around, there is another twenty-something business owner raking in the dough.

Money is important, but it does not sustain a true entrepreneur. Genuine passion, interest, curiosity and an urge to make a difference provide meaningful, enduring purpose beyond the joy of achieving wealth. Let me conclude by showing you what the most meaningful part of success is to me. It is about:

- ... becoming a lifelong advocate for minority and women-owned businesses;
- ... leading my team to areas they thought were impossible;
- ... being a devout Christian; and
- ... being a philanthropist and giving back every day.

Success is about people telling me:

- "You are such an inspiration."
- "I appreciate your honesty and transparency."
- "You have done so much for others."
- "You are an incredible speaker."
- "You are so amazing, can I call you?"

Success is about being true to yourself and leaving a legacy behind—a legacy of having enriched peoples' lives and having made a difference.

Success is out there for you to claim. What are you waiting for?

Success comes in many different forms. I have the privilege of working to increase women's participation in technology with many other successful technical women. Here are a few of their stories:

LUCY SANDERS, CEO, NCWIT

Lucy Sanders is CEO and co-founder of the National Center for Women & Information Technology (NCWIT) and also serves as Executive-in-Residence for the ATLAS Institute at the University of Colorado Boulder (CU).

Lucy has an extensive industry background, having worked in R&D and executive (VP) positions at AT&T Bell Labs, Lucent Bell Labs, and Avaya Labs for over 20 years, where she specialized in systems-level software and solutions (multi-media communication, and customer relationship management). In 1996, Lucy was awarded the Bell Labs Fellow Award, the highest technical accomplishment bestowed at the company, and she has six patents in the communications technology area.

Lucy serves as a trustee on several technology boards, including the Center for American Entrepreneurship in Washington D.C. and the International Computer Science Institute at the University of California, Berkeley. She also frequently advises young technology companies. Lucy has served on the Information Technology Research and Development Ecosystem Commission for the National Academies and the Innovation Advisory Board for the U.S. Department of Commerce.

Lucy is a recipient, along with NCWIT co-founders Robert Schnabel and Telle Whitney, of the Computing Research Association's 2012 A. Nico Habermann Award. In 2004, she was awarded the Distinguished Alumni Award from the Department of Engineering at CU, and in 2011, she was recognized with the university's George Norlin Distinguished Service Award. She has been inducted into the Women in Technology International (WITI) Hall of Fame and is a recipient of the 2013 U.S. News STEM Leadership Hall of Fame Award. Lucy received her BS and MS in computer science from Louisiana State University and the University of Colorado Boulder, respectively.

I have had the pleasure of serving with Lucy on the Board of Directors of NCWIT. She has led the organization from humble beginnings to the only national infrastructure of its kind. NCWIT is a change leader community that convenes, equips and encourages its members to effect change in their own respective organizations.

It has been a long, slow climb to get large organizations to change their cultures to make them more welcoming to women and people of color. Lucy has been the right leader, creating an amazing legacy.

NANCY PHILLIPS, CEO, VIAWEST

ViaWest is a data center and infrastructure company headquartered in Boulder, Colorado. The company has 600 employees and over 2,500 customers.

Nancy has been a successful entrepreneur for years. She used to be so ingrained in the business, touching all aspects of it, that it was hard to see some of the bigger things that were going on. She cautions that you have to stay very grounded in day-to-day execution, while at the same time, pay attention to the future.

It's been a balancing act for Nancy, determining how much time to spend on the right degree of execution and picking her head up to look further out. She's had to learn how to divide her time appropriately.

Being deeply engrained in the business, you see the industry ebbs and flows. During the dotcom bust,

Nancy saw customers going out of business on a regular basis, and it broke her heart. She wondered how she would survive the significant downturn in business.

Nancy could have gone out of business during that period. Most companies in the same data-center-centric business became very distressed and closed down. She got pushed to the brink and found herself looking over the abyss.

You only have two choices at that point—either fall over or figure out how to work your way back.

Nancy had to reorganize, take a step back, and was very fortunate to rebuild. At the end of the day, the misfortune of others became a win for her as she was able to pick up distressed assets for pennies on a dollar.

You come away from such an experience much more organized, focused and determined to run a better company.

If you have a chance to speak with most entrepreneurs, myself included, you will learn that 99 percent of successful businesses today had to weather one or more severe downturns in business to get to where we are. Nancy decided she needed to become a "T-shaped person" in order to survive.

T-shaped people have the ability to dive deeply down into their businesses to live in the product, and pop back up as a leader to transcend the cross-functional capabilities. At the top of the T, we effortlessly move across the organization. While on the vertical plane of the T, we live on the assembly line some days so we can see how our people live, dream and respond to customer demands.

Nancy focused on building her company from customer #1 to customer #2,500, staying true to her roots that got her to the point in time where she sold ViaWest in 2014 for more than $1 billion!

Business owners can become legends in their own minds if they are not careful. You have to stay humble and grounded—never take for granted your people, your customers, or the community of supporters who helped you along the way. As Nancy puts it, "Don't get too far over your skis." This helps you build a reputation of which you can be proud.

Path to exit. Nancy always had a capital-intensive business. She always had private equity sponsors along the way (who were patient in the beginning). During her struggle to move back from the abyss, she saw all the value they had built wash away during the downturn. Because of her personal sense of responsibility to all of her investors, she had to get it back. Failure was not an option.

Nancy was able to successfully enter the next private equity round. She has been keenly focused on building the company. And what gives her immense joy is that she built a company reputation that's unprecedented—a great company, with great people, who do great work.

"That's what I live for," says Nancy, "meeting the mantle of customer service and excellence. I took the company to its full potential; I can close that chapter and feel exceptional about it."

This is what success looks like!

What's next for Nancy? At the time of this writing, she wasn't sure. She, like so many other successful entrepreneurs, is involved in many things she loves. Nancy gets totally jazzed by working with new entrepreneurial women. She loves enabling, supporting and encouraging women to 1) thrive as entrepreneurs, and 2) to get involved with technology.

As one of the very few women in the world who runs a data center company, a very underserved area of the market, Nancy is also concerned about the lack of women in technology. I have the good fortune of serving on the NCWIT Board of Directors with Nancy and know first-hand how committed she is to changing this dynamic.

As a result of ViaWest's acquisition, Nancy doesn't *have* to work. She *wants* to work. She says, "I still have things on my list to do." She is still the CEO of ViaWest and is very happy working with her acquirers, the Shaw Group. "When I stop having fun, I'll do something else." That's the beauty of being in control of your own destiny.

That's what success looks and feels like!

GEORGIA PAPATHOMAS, PHD
CIO, JOHNSON & JOHNSON PHARMA

Georgia's biggest challenge on her path to success has been fighting her own insecurities and believing in herself. She has taken many risks, but always felt completely insecure in doing so. These insecurities didn't stop her from wanting to try new things, but it was a complete struggle. She needed the encouragement from her management, colleagues, and a constant source of encouragement from her husband.

She always wanted to try something different and daring, feeding her love of learning. It wasn't a simple act for Georgia. Whenever she made a big step in something new, she second-guessed herself and questioned her abilities. However, it was never bad enough to hold her back. Once she tried that "something new," she realized it really wasn't that bad, and it always worked out.

This is a pretty common condition among women, known as the "Imposter Syndrome." The social science research on this issue tells us that women, despite their extremely impressive credentials and body of work, still struggle with thinking we aren't good enough to fill a role. And that people will eventually find us out.

What kept Georgia going was the fact that every time she tried something bigger and better, she completely enjoyed it and excelled at it. She was learning something new and it was impactful for herself and society. What kept her back at times was her self-confidence. She has been able to manage it.

Over the last ten years, what has made things easier for Georgia is the fact that she has had many more role models. In the first decade of her career, she did not see women in roles to which she could aspire. In her environment, there were all men—no women. As a result, it was impossible to see someone like herself who made it.

Georgia came to the United States from Greece by herself to attend college. While that took a lot of courage, she didn't know what she was really getting herself into. Because she was able to survive in a challenging environment and school setting (Columbia University in New York City), she didn't know at the time the real challenges that were to face her.

As she puts it, many people in school can get an A. However, there's only one person in industry who can occupy the top spot or get the next promotion.

She always looked at the excitement of the job requirements, and not her capabilities. She pursued new roles based on her level of excitement, and second-guessed her actions based on her insecurities.

Georgia is driven by a vision. If any job didn't elicit a vision for something bigger, she didn't go after it. She had to be inspired in order to battle her insecurities. It didn't matter if the new role impacted the world or just one person. If she was inspired, she summoned up all the energy needed to overcome her insecurities.

Georgia's mother was her chief source of inspiration. She was one of those women who didn't see a difference between men and women. She painted for Georgia a vision of the world where women were doctors and presidents of countries. She would talk to her and her friends to imagine themselves becoming doctors, taking care of hundreds of people. Or she would envision Georgia as an engineer, building the most intricate of bridges. That is how she talked to her children.

Georgia's mother, clearly ahead of her time, was intentional about speaking this truth into Georgia and her friends so they could internalize it. She didn't say, "You could do it if you tried." Instead, she would tell the girls she could "see" them in these roles.

She could see what success looked like!

Georgia never heard Cinderella-type stories from her mother—only stories about the great things the girls would ultimately accomplish. She did a great work in these girls.

Had other women and people of color been fed these visionary realities, would we still have the dearth of women in tech that we have now?

It's clear—painting a picture with girls and people of color reflected in it—goes a long way in instilling the belief of what is possible. This can come from parents or others close to you.

There are also not enough role models. People think because we have had an African-American president, we have arrived. But that is far from the truth.

Some actually believe we have come a long way and there is no reason to go the extra mile. But, we are nowhere close to having the representation equivalent to our percentage of the population.

Georgia's encouragement: *Dream big, set high goals for yourself and believe you can accomplish them.* Even if you feel insecure, believe that if you try, you can do it. Stick up for yourself. You own your future—don't let others dictate it. Remember, it takes an effort. It's not going to happen without really trying hard.

There is nothing wrong with asking for help. There's nothing wrong with saying, "I don't know." No one knows everything, so there is no stigma attached to "I don't know." For some reason, women are afraid to admit we don't know things, especially in a male-dominated environment. We are afraid of appearing unknowledgeable, whether in class or a work environment. As a result, we miss opportunities to learn.

Think of asking questions as a learning opportunity instead of appearing unknowledgeable. Stop worrying about how it appears.

Having women in the business is no longer a nice thing to do; it is a business imperative. Women are bringing value to every organization. We need to own that power.

This is what success looks like!

CHAPTER 11

SIT WITH ME!

*Courage is what it takes to stand and speak;
courage is also what it takes to
sit down and listen.*

A round 2011, the idea for the NCWIT outreach and marketing campaign was born. "Sit With Me" is its name. It was designed to get people talking about the lack of women designing the technology we all depend on every day. We realized we needed to broaden the conversation and had to create a vehicle with which to do so.

"Sit With Me" resonated with me right from the very beginning. I wasn't sure why until I delved a little deeper. And then it hit me!

Providing access and opportunities for women and people of color to participate in the growing tech industry was similar to every other civil rights struggle of the past. We are not at the table, we are not sought after, our voices aren't being heard, and we are not partakers of any of the wealth that is being created in the tech industry.

So, the idea was somewhat akin to the event that sparked the civil rights movement.

When Rosa Parks sat her tired self down on a front seat of that bus in Montgomery, Alabama in 1955, she did so knowing full well her actions would inevitably incite a negative response. But she decided to sit in the front anyway. She was just too tired to keep moving to the back; and why should she? Did she not pay her hard-earned money for a seat on that bus just like all the other riders?

Her courage to face the sure-to-come backlash empowered her to take a stand to end the poor treatment of working class Black people everywhere.

By doing so, she started a movement that changed the world. Her quiet courage sparked a similar resolve in others to demand inclusion, fight for the right to vote and go to schools that were formerly off limits; and unfortunately in many cases, to die for the right to be free.

That same indomitable spirit and resolve is what is needed today to open the floodgates of opportunity and ensure people who have been left out of the tech craze and the wealth generated by it, finally get a seat at the table.

"Sit With Me" is a national advocacy campaign designed to encourage women in computing careers. The campaign seeks to raise the visibility of technical women by providing a gathering place for people (men, women, technical, non-technical) to acknowledge the valuable contributions of women in computing.

"Sit With Me" uses an iconic red chair to symbolize that women in technology need more seats at the table, that men and women can sit in support and solidarity for technical women, and that one highly visible action can instigate others.

The campaign's underlying premise is actually a call to action ...

- Sit with me to take a stand for technical women.
- Sit with me in support of technical women.
- Sit with me to increase women's and people of color's meaningful participation in computing.
- We need more "seats" at the design table.
- We won't stand for anything less!

The "ask" is simple, yet symbolic. We ask everyone, everywhere to sit in the red chair, tell us your story and how you can become a catalyst for change.

The idea so resonated with me, that I requested to become the National Spokesperson of the Sit With Me Campaign. I was readily granted that request and have been serving in this capacity for several years now.

I spend a good deal of time helping companies define ways to increase the visibility of technical women within their organization by staging internal Sit With Me events. Or, how to add a Sit With Me component to an upcoming event they are planning for their employee base or community at large.

It has been an amazing experience serving in this capacity and helping to spread the important message of fairness and equity all across the country. I have been involved with countless successful events and have gained a lot of satisfaction knowing my efforts are making a difference in the world.

Many notable celebrities and senior executives have been photographed sitting in the red chair. And the chair has been spotted at such iconic places as the Martin Luther King, Jr. Memorial in Washington, DC, at the Reflecting Pool, also in Washington, DC, with the Rocky Mountains in the background, and in the cockpit of a United 737 jetliner.

All we're asking is that you spend a few minutes sharing your story—your influences and inspirations, and the challenges and opportunities you see for the future.

My burning desire is to increase the visibility of the issue of the lack of our participation in tech by shining a brighter light on the Red Chair. It would be great if its symbolism became as well known and fully embraced as other symbols—like the pink ribbon for breast cancer, for example.

HOW DO WE GET THERE?

To accomplish that objective, several things will have to happen:

- We need to reach the appropriate level of funding to produce a mainstream media campaign. The amount is minimally $1 million a year.
- We will have to identify and secure one or more National Presenting Sponsors—ideally, a corporation with an iconic brand of its own that we could leverage to heighten the awareness of the problem and potential solutions.
- We would need to gain access to major media outlets.
- It would be important to encourage a well-respected, notable celebrity to become the "face of tech equality."
- It is critical that we build a sustainable model to ensure we can achieve continuity and advance the cause year over year.

We *can* do this. It is such important work, that failure is not an option.

I am personally invested in this cause because I see the potential to change lives and hopefully leave a legacy—a positive impact that will live on long after I'm gone ... a tangible example of paying it forward and charting a path that others can follow.

Help us send the message that attracting, retaining and promoting technical women are critical for success at every company across the U.S.

So, sit down!

Have a seat! Grab a chair!

Sit with me!!

Here are some memorable moments from the road ...

The author and the Red Chair in different venues
as part of the "Sit With Me" campaign.

Kim Stevenson
Former CIO
Intel Corporation

Elizabeth A. Dinndorf, J.D.
President, Columbia College

Pauline Gabon
Supply Diversity Director,
MetLife, Inc.

Carla Franklin
Java Programmer
CEO, Carlin Solutions

Lyria Charles
Former Chief of Staff,
TCGi

The Red Chair

The author (2nd from left) participating in the White House Summit on Working Families

The Red Chair in the data center of Via West

Shaquille O'Neill dwarfing the Red Chair

There are many others who elect to sit in
support of technical women ...

And millions more to come...

How about you? Will you have a seat?
Sit down with me and let's talk IT.
We can solve this problem if we work together.

RESOURCES AND REFERENCES

BlackGirlsCode: www.blackgirlscode.com

Code: www.code.org

Girls Who Code: www.girlswhocode.com

Grace Hopper Celebration of Women in Computing: http://ghc.anitaborg.org/

National Center for Women & Information Technology: www.ncwit.org

NCWIT Aspirations in Computing: www.aspirations.org

Project Implicit: www.Projectimplicit.com

Sit With Me Campaign: www.sitwithme.org

Society of Women Engineers: http://societyofwomenengineers.swe.org/

Technolochicas: http://technolochicas.org/

Women in Technology International: https://www.witi.com/

REFERENCES

Brown, M., Setren, E., Topa, G.. "Do Informal Referrals Lead to Better Matches? Evidence from a Firm's Employee Referral System." Federal Reserve Bank Staff Report, no. 568, 2012 – revised 2013. https://www.newyorkfed.org/medialibrary/media/research/staff_reports/sr568.pdf

Herring, Cedric. "Does Diversity Pay?: Race, Gender, and the Business Case for Diversity." *American Sociological Review.* vol. 74, no. 2, 2009, pp. 208-204. http://asr.sagepub.com/content/74/2/208.short

Lanker, Brian. *I Dream a World: Portraits of Black Women Who Changed America.* New York: Stewart Tabori & Chang, 1989. https://www.abebooks.com/9781556709234/Dream-World-Portraits-Black-Women-1556709234/plp

London Business School: The Lehman Centre for Women in Business. "Innovative Potential: Men and Women in Teams." 2008 http://communications.london.edu/aem/

clients/LBS001/docs/lehman/November_%
202007_Innovative_Potential_Men_and_Women_in_Tea
ms.pdf

Page, Scott E. *The Difference: How the Power of Diversity Creates Better Groups, Firms, Schools, and Societies.* Princeton: Princeton University Press, 2007.

United States Census Bureau. http://www.census.gov/topics/income-poverty/income.

United States Department of Bureau and Labor Statistics: Labor Force Statistics from the Current Population Survey. http://www.bls.gov/cps/cpsaat11.htm

Wagstaff, Keith. "Can We Fix Computer Science Education in America?." *TIME* Magazine, 16 July 2012. http://techland.time.com/2012/07/16/can-we-fix-computer-science-education-in-america/

Woolley, Anita Williams, et al. "Evidence for a Collective Intelligence Factor in the Performance of Human Groups." *Science.* vol. 330, 2010, pp. 686-688. https://www.cs.cmu.edu/~ab/Salon/research/Woolley_et_al_Science_2010-2.pdf

Zickuhr, Kathryn. "Who's Not Online and Why". Pew Research Center, 2013. http://www.pewinternet.org/2013/09/25/whos-not-online-and-why/

Zimmerman, Michael. "The Facts About Outsourcing and the U.S. Economy, and What They Mean for Your Business". SmartCEO.com. http://www.smartceo.com/the-facts-about-outsourcing-and-the-u-s-economy-and-what-they-mean-for-your-business/

ACKNOWLEDGMENTS

I have been so encouraged to write this book by my family, friends and professional associates alike. It's been a long time coming, but it's finally here, and I thank God for blessing me to complete it.

Special thanks to my husband and biggest supporter, Robert Rivers, who even gifted me with the technology to speak the book into existence!

My children, Tonya, and Jamel, and stepdaughters, Nikki, Chanelle and Taigi. My daughter-in-law, Amber and son-in-law, Nelson. All of them combined have blessed us with ten grandchildren—Khyree, Cairo, Moses, Darnell, Cameron, Miracle, Trinity, Elijah, Savanna, and Zara.

My family has been a tremendous support throughout the years in so many ways. My mother, Annie, has always been my #1 Fan, and I will be forever grateful. My sisters, Karen, Ondria, and Mira, and sisters-in-law, Anita and Claudia, have shown nothing but love and concern for me, my well-being, guarding my soul and keeping it real. Thank you, my sisters.

Thank you to my brothers as well—Darrell, John, Zo and Fate, for being strong encouragers and not so manly that it prevented you from showering me with love.

To my large extended family of aunts, uncles, cousins, nieces and nephews—thank you for your love and encouragement along my journey.

My long-time friend, Rohena Miller, has been encouraging me to write this book for more than a decade, and I had a great example of how to get it done by watching my BFF, Mikki Taylor, complete three successful books. Thank you both for being my "Ride or Die" for more years than any of us want to admit.

Thank you, Black Pearls—you keep me grounded, enveloped with love, and true to myself. I can never bluff my way past you; you won't let me!

To my partners in the struggle—Brad, Lucy, Paula, Kay, Ruthe, Catherine, Casey, the Board, and everyone at NCWIT. You've provided me with the context, research, passion and determination to see it through to the end. You're doing incredible work and I am humbled and honored to be partnered with you.

To my Garretson Road family—you keep me steady, reminding me what's truly important, and to stay true to God. You encourage me, pray for me, scold me when you think I'm overdoing it, and just pick me up when I fall. Thank you for the unconditional love. I couldn't do what I do without it.

And, finally, to my incredible team at TCGi, who holds it down, has my back, and allows me to pursue my passion to make a difference in this world. I couldn't do it without you; I love each and every one of you. Thank you.

There are so many more I could and should thank, but that would be another book all by itself. Suffice it to say that so many have touched my life and I am a better person because of it.

THANK YOU!

ABOUT THE AUTHOR

Avis Yates Rivers is a 32-year Tech CEO. After a successful 11-year career at Exxon, she decided to branch out on her own and blaze a trail for others to follow. She felt growing up one of six children in New York City prepared her well for the challenge. Having spent the last five years of her corporate career selling early technology to firms in lower Manhattan also provided a platform from which she could launch a business to continue to service Exxon's customers. Exxon had sold the Office Systems division, which left a temporary void in the marketplace. So, in January of 1985, Avis founded her first tech firm.

Even at a young age, her vision allowed her to see what was possible. She was already familiar with hard work, and was willing to do what was necessary to succeed. Three decades later, she has accomplished a great deal and leaves a strong legacy in the world of business.

Avis has reached the point in her career where she feels it is important to be "in service." She believes deeply in the late Shirley Chisholm's ideal that "service is the rent you pay for the privilege of living on this earth." Avis is a long-time advocate for the increased utilization of minority and women-owned businesses, and a change agent for increasing the meaningful participation of women and people of color in technology. She serves as a director on the boards of a select group of non-profit organizations, and is the National Spokesperson for NCWIT's "Sit With Me" Campaign.

Avis is the recipient of numerous awards, honors and recognition bestowed on her over the years, and is the embodiment of a strong faith, hard work and a lot of help along the way.